D1161562

Dryden and the Art of Translation

by William Frost

ASSISTANT PROFESSOR OF ENGLISH, SANTA BARBARA COLLEGE

ARCHON BOOKS 1969

Copyright, 1955, by Yale University Press
Reprinted 1969 with permission of Yale University Press
in an unaltered and unabridged edition

[*Yale Studies in English, Vol. 128*]

SBN: 208 00778 4
Library of Congress Catalog Card Number: 69-15684
Printed in the United States of America

To J. W. and C. G. F.

Preface

I N P U B L I S H I N G the following study of Dryden, it is pleasant to have the opportunity of acknowledging a number of debts. I am grateful to Harcourt, Brace for permission to quote a passage from Stephen Spender's *World within World;* to Dodd, Mead & Co. for permission to quote from Leacock's *Laugh with Leacock;* and to Henry Holt & Co. for permission to quote Housman's "Diffugere Nives"; also to Joseph McGrath James Bottkol, whose unpublished Harvard dissertation, "Dryden's Translations from Classical Verse" (1937), and published work based on that dissertation have established the right of Dryden's scholarship to be taken seriously; to the late George R. Noyes for data contained in his admirable Cambridge edition of Dryden's poems; to Yale University for awarding the John Addison Porter Prize to the doctoral dissertation out of which the present book has grown; to Emma H. E. Stephenson of the Yale Library; to the University of California for underwriting, through Santa Barbara College, various expenses in connection with preparing the manuscript; to Douglas Knight for *Pope and the Heroic Tradition,* and for many conversations, not soon to be forgotten, about Homer, the Augustans, and other subjects; to Maynard Mack, inspirer and critic of my work on Dryden, director of the original dissertation, unfailing counsellor and friend; and to my dear wife, who has often consented to hear these pages read aloud.

Contents

I

Introduction

A S A POET—apart, that is, from his plays and his prose criticism—Dryden devoted most of his energies to translation. Even if we include among the nondramatic original poems his numerous prologues and epilogues for the theater, it still remains true that in sheer bulk the translations make up approximately two-thirds of all his poetry. For every line of original nondramatic poetry he wrote two lines of translation from a foreign poet.

Far from being apprentice work, Dryden's translations were, for his contemporaries at least, the climax of his poetic career. More than nine-tenths of them—measured, again, in sheer number of lines—were published during the last decade of his life, and these include his most mature and impressive work in the genre: the Juvenal and Persius in 1692; the complete Virgil in 1697, and the selections from Chaucer, Ovid, Boccaccio, and Homer in the *Fables* volume of 1700, the year of his death. The Virgil, which appears to have consumed the labor of about four years, is itself as long as all Dryden's original poetry put together. Of his best translations, only the bits of Horace and Lucretius in the *Sylvae* anthology of 1685 were published before 1690; all the rest fall within the final decade.

There were, of course, economic, sociological, and political reasons why Dryden's time should have been given to translation especially after 1688, when the fall of the Restoration monarchy made his theatrical career less certain of success and his career as satirist and propagandist out of the question entirely. The importance of his subsequent translations to literature as a career for men of talent has been, since the publication in 1881 of Alexandre Beljame's lively and stimulating study,[1] widely understood. In Dryden's youth—just as formerly in the Elizabethan age—an aspiring poet could hope for an income from the theater or from patronage; in Dryden's middle years, at the time of the controversy over the succession in the '80s, a third source of revenue became available to political propagandists, authors of works like *Absalom and Achitophel;* and all three of these resources—stage, patronage, and propaganda—involved dependence on small aristocratic, or at least po-

1. *Men of Letters and the English Public in the Eighteenth Century, 1660–1744, Dryden, Addison, Pope;* ed. Bonamy Dobrée, tr. E. O. Lorimer (Routledge and Kegan Paul, 1948). See especially pp. 354–86, the concluding section of the volume.

litically powerful, groups. At the end of the century, however, working in collaboration with the pioneering publisher Jacob Tonson, Dryden was able to take effective advantage of the presence of a new body of readers, and to appeal directly to his public without the mediation of theater manager, patron, or politician. This was the public that would later grant the young Pope—whom Tories called a Whig and Whigs a Tory—lifelong independence as a reward for translating Homer and editing Shakespeare. It was also the public that ensured the success of the *Spectator* papers only a few years after Dryden's death; that supported the great novelists of the later eighteenth century; and that ultimately enabled Samuel Johnson to regard patronage as an obsolete institution.

As is well known, this public was heavily bourgeois; and there are indications that its literacy, in practice, was confined largely to the native tongue. The *Spectator* occasionally printed jokes about readers who failed to interpret correctly—or to explain correctly to enquiring females —the Greek or Latin mottoes which adorned each issue. A mention of Greeks and Trojans at an officers' mess in *Tom Jones* elicits a vociferous protest from one of the young ensigns present:

> "D——n Homo with all my heart," says Northerton; "I have the marks of him on my a—— yet. There's Thomas, of our regiment, always carries a Homo in his pocket; d——n me, if ever I come at it, if I don't burn it."

The poet Prior put a similar complaint more elegantly than Ensign Northerton:

> Hang HOMER and VIRGIL; their meaning to seek,
> A Man must have pok'd in the *Latin* and *Greek;*
> Those who Love their own Tongue, we have Reason to Hope,
> Have read them Translated by DRYDEN and POPE.

To the career of verse translator, for so various but not always learned a public, Dryden brought unusual talents and qualifications. The recipient of a sound classical education at the ungentle hands of the bludgeoning Dr. Busby, he continued to read widely in foreign literature throughout his life, and to study European criticism both ancient and modern. At the same time his career in the theater—and particularly his

2. Dryden's profits from his Virgil came (a) from 351 subscribers, whose names were printed at the back of the first edition (£390); (b) from Tonson directly (£200); and (c) from patrons (dedicatees, etc.), who may have contributed up to £1,000. See C. E. Ward, "The Publication and Profits of Dryden's Virgil," *PMLA, 53* (1938); 807–12. (Thirty years earlier Milton's publisher paid him £10 for *Paradise Lost.*) We may then figure Dryden's income from his Virgil at about £400 a year during the four years he worked on it; two decades later, Pope spent eight or nine years on his *Iliad* and *Odyssey* and made about £10,000 in all.

heavy output of prologues and epilogues for other dramatists' plays as well as for his own—had given him a command of easy, colloquial verse unequaled by any English poet since Shakespeare's time. He knew the accents of the spoken tongue; yet he brought to the classics a scholar's passion:

> He sat with a favorite edition open before him (Prateus, Ruaeus, Casaubon, or Cnipping), read the original carefully, often the Latin prose *Interpretatio,* and invariably studied the accompanying annotations. When he came to a difficult or disputed passage, he repeatedly turned to other editors, studied and compared their varying opinions, and then chose to follow one authority or another or even to make a new interpretation for himself. Also he had open before him on the table one or more earlier English translations, particularly those which were written in heroic couplets. From these he often took rhymes, stray phrases, even whole lines and passages.[3]

Dryden's use of these earlier translations has sometimes drawn a smile, or a reproof for his laziness, from later critics. Actually, as he was well aware, he began his work at the end of a century of experimentation with the Englishing of foreign poets; and it would have been as foolish for him not to investigate his predecessors as it was impossible for him to remain wholly uninfluenced by what he found to be their occasional successes. To take for example Virgil's *Georgics,* for which Dryden's indebtedness in this respect has been studied in detail,[4] there were at least nine earlier complete or partial translations which Dryden might have seen; and he is known to have adopted some nineteen different lines, with no change or almost none, from several of his translating forebears —as well as a larger number of phrases, pairs of rhyme words, etc. Nineteen complete lines out of the 3,149 in Dryden's version is not indicative of a heavy debt, certainly; but it shows his sense of his own work as the culmination of a tradition—which indeed it was.

How has this tradition fared among later readers?

In the two and a half centuries since Dryden's death his *Aeneid* and his Chaucer have attracted more critical comment than all his other translations combined, the *Aeneid* doubtless because of its scope and its mag-

---

3. Quoted from J. M. J. Bottkol's "Dryden's Latin Scholarship," *Modern Philology,* 40 (1943), 243. This is a pioneering study of Dryden's responsibility to his originals; it conclusively refutes the charges of carelessness or ignorance sometimes formerly brought against Dryden. "If the contemporary authorities on which Dryden himself relied are compared with the translations," Bottkol writes, "it at once becomes clear that, in all but a small number of examples, his departures from the original are due to aesthetic or stylistic reasons—not to ignorance or imperfect knowledge of Latin."

4. See H. M. Hooker, "Dryden's *Georgics* and English Predecessors," *Huntington Library Quarterly, 9* (1945–46), 273–310; also the comment on this article by Bottkol in *Philological Quarterly, 26* (1947), 118–19.

nificence, the Chaucer partly because of the increasing interest among English readers in Chaucer himself.

On the whole, the reputation of his *Aeneid* has been the more stable of the two. The enthusiasm of an early critic who wrote:

> let who will undertake that *Mighty Work* [of translating Virgil], we shall never see it better perform'd in the Whole; and those who may excel him, where they observe that he hath failed, will fall below him in a Thousand Instances where he hath excelled.[5]

finds an echo today in the judgments of Stuart Bates:

> I came to make these comparisons [of Dryden with other Virgil translators] with a prejudice against Dryden; I came away with the conviction that his merits as a translator of Virgil surpass all those of his fellow translators put together; that, whatever Modern Translation may add in detail, or alternative, it has not been able to supersede, or even rival, Dryden, book for book.[6]

and of Douglas Bush:

> no English critic has shown more sympathetic insight into the mind and art of Virgil than Dryden. . . . Dryden's Virgil, with all the inadequacies that have been observed, is in its general texture a splendid achievement. I may say that my own experience was parallel to that lately reported by Mr. Stuart Bates.[7]

Among its other admirers Dryden's Virgil has numbered Sir Walter Scott[8] ("the ancient poet's ideas with force and energy equal to his own"), John Conington[9] ("Compare him with other translators and it will seem that while none of them have anything of Virgil's individuality, he alone has an individuality of his own of sufficient mark to interest and impress the reader"), Sir Edmund Gosse[1] ("no more satisfactory translation, as English poetry, has ever been produced"), Mark Van Doren[2] ("still has more vitality than any other translation"); and, with reservations, John Churton Collins[3] ("a work instinct with genius; . . .

---

5. Henry Felton, *A Dissertation on Reading the Classics . . . Written in the Year 1709* (4th ed., 1730), pp. 129–30.

6. *Modern Translation* (Oxford Univ. Press, 1936), p. 29.

7. *Mythology and Romantic Tradition in English Poetry* (Harvard Univ. Press, 1937), pp. 6, 17. Bush would, however, make an exception in favor of Gavin Douglas' sixteenth-century Middle Scots *Eneados,* which has also been preferred to Dryden's version by Robert Bridges (see his *Ibant Obscuri* [Clarendon Press, 1916], p. 139).

8. *Life of Dryden* (Vol. 2 in Scott-Saintsbury edition of Dryden's *Works,* 1882), p. 432.

9. John Conington, "English Translations of Virgil," *Quarterly Review, 110* (1861), 96.

1. *A History of Eighteenth-Century Literature* (1889), p. 70.

2. *Poetry of Dryden* (Henry Holt, 1946), p. 255.

3. *Essays and Studies* (1895), pp. 70, 77.

he had been able . . . to substitute a masterpiece of rhetoric for a masterpiece of poetry"), George Saintsbury [4] ("Dryden has done him excellently . . . only that the spirit of the translation is entirely different from that of the original"), and George Stuart Gordon:

> Dryden, as Johnson remarked, is not one of the "gentle bosoms," and much of the delicacy and *desiderium* of Virgil escapes him. But his translation remains by almost general consent what Lord Bowen, a rival translator, has called it: "the noblest and most masculine of all the versions" . . . Dryden's Virgil became at once a substantive part of English literature, one of the greater English poems, and Virgil entered the eighteenth century an English citizen.[5]

In the minority camp, Wordsworth ("whenever Virgil can be fairly said to have his *eye* upon his object, Dryden always spoils the passage" [6]) is still the most famous objector; though time has not been kind to Wordsworth's own partial translation of Virgil, which a twentieth-century critic calls "far flatter and more conventional than the flattest parts of Dryden." [7]

The case of Dryden's versions of Chaucer [8] is more complex. They fared well in the eighteenth century, being widely approved, reprinted, and imitated.[9] Inspired by Dryden, Pope translated two more of the Canterbury poems; two extensive modernized versions of the *Tales,* produced by Ogle (1741) and Lipscomb (1795), included Dryden's work in whole or in large part; and Thomas Warton, in his *History of English Poetry* (1774), pronounced "Palamon and Arcite" "the most animated and harmonious piece of versification in the English language." [1]

Even in the nineteenth century admirers were not entirely lacking. John ("Christopher North") Wilson considered the new "Knight's Tale" "a great modern poem" and George Saintsbury thought that it would "even bear the strain of comparison" to the original.[2] But such

---

4. *Dryden* (1930; 1st ed., 1881), p. 147.
5. *Virgil in English Poetry* (Humphrey Milford, 1931), p. 12.
6. *Early Letters of William and Dorothy Wordsworth*, ed. E. de Selincourt (Clarendon Press, 1935), letter to Scott (Nov. 7, 1805), p. 541.
7. T. H. Warren, *Essays of Poets and Poetry, Ancient and Modern* (Murray, 1909), p. 86.
8. These comprise (1) "Palamon and Arcite" (from "The Knight's Tale"), (2) "The Cock and the Fox" (from "The Nun's Priest's Tale"), (3) "The Wife of Bath, Her Tale," (4) "The Flower and the Leaf" (from a Middle English poem then mistakenly attributed to Chaucer), and (5) "The Character of a Good Parson" (adapted and greatly expanded from the portrait of the parson in the Prologue). Critical attention has focused on the first three of these.
9. For details see H. G. Wright, "Some Sidelights on the Reputation and Influence of Dryden's *Fables,*" *Review of English Studies, 21* (1945), 23–37.
1. *1, 367.*
2. For Wilson see *Blackwood's Magazine, 57* (1845), 785. For Saintsbury see his *Dryden,* p. 158.

judgments were heterodox in that age. First there was the revolution in taste caused by the Romantics. "Chaucer," Wordsworth wrote to Scott in 1808, "I think he [Dryden] has entirely spoiled, even wantonly deviating from his great original, and always for the worse." [3] Second, there was the rediscovery of more authentic texts of Chaucer than Dryden knew, and of the proper way to pronounce them; something like bardolatry followed. "All that is good in Dryden, with few, if any, exceptions, belongs to Chaucer; and all that is bad in Dryden is his own unquestionable property," wrote a certain John Saunders in 1845, basing his verdict on an unflagging veneration for every syllable of the original.[4] Out of a similar deference Alexander Smith advocated and practiced "the medium of prose" for translating Chaucer; and ventured the judgment that "Dryden and Pope did not translate or modernize Chaucer, —they committed assault and battery upon him." [5] Toward the close of the century the Chaucerian scholar Lounsbury, although deprecating Smith's rancor and asserting that Dryden was being undervalued, nevertheless gave several pages to a new catalogue of objections to details of Dryden's work; and John Churton Collins in 1895 found Dryden's failure with Chaucer "deplorable." [6] More recently A. E. Housman, inspired by the same critical tradition, poured caustic scorn on Dryden's Chaucer before an Oxford audience of 1933. The eighteenth century, he remarked with irritation, invented for poetry a "correct and splendid diction" which "consisted in always using the wrong word instead of the right"; and Augustan poets, according to him, "plastered it as ornament, with no thought of propriety, on whatever they desired to dignify." [7]

Except for Housman, however, twentieth-century critics have been more guarded. Allardyce Nicoll, A. A. Jack, A. W. Verrall, and Mark Van Doren have found elements to admire in Dryden's translations from Middle English—though always with reservations, and without unanimity among themselves as to which of these works are most successful. Nicoll speaks of them, in general, as "real triumphs" and sees "nothing fundamentally wrong" in Dryden's "attempt to interpret and adapt" the older poet.[8] Verrall, Jack, and Van Doren agree in liking "The Cock and the Fox," but disagree as to the merits of "Palamon and Arcite"; for "The Wife of Bath, Her Tale" there has been less enthusiasm.[9]

Two critical problems, one general and one specific, are suggested,

3. *Letters (1806–11)*, ed. de Selincourt (1937), p. 458c.
4. Saunders, *The Canterbury Tales* (1845–47), *2*, 135. See also *1*, 82 ff., 155 ff.; *2*, 131 ff.
5. *Dreamthorp* (1863), p. 232.
6. Lounsbury, *Studies in Chaucer* (1892), *3*, 161; Collins, *Essays and Studies*, p. 77.
7. *Name and Nature of Poetry* (Macmillan, 1933), pp. 18–19.
8. *Dryden and His Poetry* (1923), pp. 100, 104.
9. See Jack, *A Commentary . . . on Chaucer and Spenser* (Maclehose, Jackson, 1920), pp. 127–30; Verrall, *Lectures on Dryden* (Cambridge Univ. Press, 1914), pp. 4, 23; and Van Doren, *Poetry of Dryden* (1946; first ed. 1920), pp. 223, 226–8.

it seems to me, by the fluctuations of Dryden's reputation as a translator. The first involves the nature of translation itself; the second, the precise relationship of Dryden's work in this field both to his originals and to other translations of them. Stated in its broadest terms, the first problem might be phrased: Can verse translation have *any* esthetic validity? The extreme attacks on Dryden's Chaucer, for example, turn out on inspection to be based on the implied premise that once Chaucer had put words on paper in a certain order, any attempt at verse translation was from that moment almost certainly doomed to failure; and if this is true for Chaucer, why not for Homer, Virgil, Lucretius, etc.—poets of comparable, or greater, stature? This is a question, moreover, in which not only Dryden is involved but all the English translators since Surrey and Chapman, and specifically all the many verse translators of the present age. It is a question which strikes me as so basic, not only for students of Dryden but also for lovers of poetry in general, that I have devoted a chapter to discussing it from the broadest point of view; and I have called this book *Dryden and the Art of Translation* to indicate that it has, in a sense, a double subject.

The second problem, that of the relation of Dryden's translations to their originals, has of course many facets; central to it, however, is the question whether Dryden's work as a translator is to be awarded an absolute, or a merely relative, value. On the one hand, as we have seen in connection with Dryden's Virgil, there is a substantial body of informed critical opinion willing to give his version of the *Aeneid* the palm over most or all other contenders, *before or since;* on the other hand, there exists a feeling that his versions pertain most of all to the age in which they appeared ("Virgil entered the eighteenth century an English citizen"). Those who assert Dryden's absolute merits sometimes do so with some lack of specification as to the exact qualities of his excellence. For example, the most recent study of his relation to earlier translators concludes that "his borrowings are woven into a single fabric, and one only needs to examine his predecessors to discover the superior grace and beauty of that fabric"; [1] but the study itself is concerned with establishing the indebtedness rather than the superiority. Those who agree with another recent student of the Virgil that Dryden "wrote within a convention which demanded . . . greater license in translation than is now permissible" [2] raise the same problem in another form. Granted that verse translation is possible at all, is its success in practice limited to the conventions of the particular age in which it occurs? Or can we compare, with the hope of arriving at useful value judgments, two translations of the same foreign poem, one written in the seventeenth, another in the twentieth century?

1. Hooker, "Dryden's *Georgics* and English Predecessors," p. 310.
2. Bottkol, "Dryden's Latin Scholarship," p. 253.

For reasons I hope to clarify in Chapter II, I believe that we can, and should, make such comparisons; and in Chapters III and IV, I shall accordingly juxtapose certain passages from Dryden with the same passages as rendered by earlier or later translators. These two final chapters are meant to demonstrate Dryden's methods, strengths, and limitations as a translator, as I understand them; and the demonstration will be carried out chiefly in connection with particular passages, such as can be subjected to fairly close examination. In general, the two final chapters proceed from smaller to larger units of poetic construction—from single word, line, couplet, or verse paragraph (in Chapter III) to certain complete works, or longer fragments (in Chapter IV) ; but it is, of course, often impossible to discuss even a short passage without some reference to the larger context in which it is embedded. I have not attempted (a labor which I think would involve much repetition) to survey all of Dryden's translations, one by one, in chronological or in some other order ; rather I have picked out what seemed to me salient features of his technique, features which recur throughout his work in this field. In doing this I find I have quoted most frequently from his Chaucer and his Virgil, and not at all from his Horace, Boccaccio, Theocritus, or Persius (works which I have, however, examined). The prospect for any student of Dryden as a translator is a wide one; and the aim of this study is exploratory.

II

Theory of Translation

1. The Theoretical Impossibility of Translation

THE BASIC ASSUMPTIONS of modern criticism make it clear that, on a priori grounds, the translation of poetry is a theoretical impossibility. In his recent autobiography *World within World*,[1] Stephen Spender discriminates between prose and verse in the following manner:

> Prose is language used in such a way that the ideas and events or scene within the language are referred to as objects existing apart from the language, so that there is an understanding between the writer and the reader that these things could be discussed in quite other words than those used, because they exist independently of the words. But directly the language tends to create, as it were, verbal objects inseparable from the words used, then the direction of the language is poetic. It is moving towards a condition where, as in poetry, the words appear to become the object, so that they cannot be replaced by other words than the ones used to convey the same experience.

Literary art depends ultimately on the words which embody it; and a word, since it is more than simply an arbitrary symbol for some object or idea, but has in itself certain qualities—its sounds when spoken, the connotations that have clustered around it in the course of its history—can never be represented, in any real sense, by an "equivalent" word, either in the same language or in another one. "No two words are precise equivalents," said that well-known Victorian translator Jowett, in a preface to his *Dialogues of Plato*, "just as no two leaves of the forest are exactly similar."

A poem, as critics since Coleridge have often pointed out, is an *organic synthesis* of words, each word being carefully chosen, if the poem is a good one, for what it can do both in its immediate context and in relation to the entire poem. The "meaning" of a poem is the poem itself; not the sum of the meanings of the words in it, but the effect produced by the complex interrelationship of the words. These will often be interrelated quite as much through sound, word order, and connotation as through their "meanings" (as a dictionary might give them) taken separately

1. New York, Harcourt, Brace; (London, Hamish Hamilton, 1951), pp. 284-5.

from each other. To imagine that anything else might be true is to be found guilty, to use a current critical term, of "the heresy of paraphrase."

Suppose for a moment that we were to take an ode by Keats, or a sonnet by Shakespeare, and for every important word in it were to substitute another English word, the closest equivalent we could find. Would the result be a replica or a facsimile of the ode or sonnet, or a substitute for it—something that would do just about as well? Yet translation, or one step in translation, at any rate, is bound to consist of just such a process, only with words in another language. It is absolutely certain, then, that the first result of translating at all is that the organic synthesis which was the original poem is utterly and inevitably shattered.

That such should be the case, discerning writers on the subject have realized, of course, for a long time. Dryden, for example, saw it clearly enough, and stated it in the dedication to his *Aeneid* as follows (he is speaking of Virgil) : "His words are not only chosen, but the places in which he ranks them, for the sound. He who removes them from the station wherein their master set them, spoils the harmony. What he says of the Sibyl's prophecies may be as properly applied to every word of his : they must be read in order as they lie ; the least breath discomposes them ; and somewhat of their divinity is lost." [2]

2. *The Nature of Actual Translation*

Despite its theoretical impossibility, the prevalence of verse translation raises an interesting question as to what anything calling itself by such a name can or should be. The question arises not only for Dryden's age but for ours. The huge extent of modern European poetic translation, both in England and on the Continent, has been vividly set forth by Ernest Stuart Bates in his two books, *Modern Translation* (1936) and *Intertraffic* (1943) ; while in the United States the last ten or twenty years have seen the appearance of new translations, mostly in verse, of such authors as Villon, Baudelaire, Mallarmé, Heine, Rilke, George, Pushkin, Lorca, Catullus, Pindar ; and of such works as the *Divine Comedy, Faust,* the *Iliad,* Aeschylus' *Agamemnon,* among many others. In England, since the appearance of Bates' more recent book, Penguin has launched a series of cheap pocket versions of a number of classics, each newly translated by a contemporary author ; of those that have so

2. Cf. Edmond Scherer, *Études sur la littérature contemporaine* (Paris, Lévy Frères, 1878) : "Deux choses font obstacle à la traduction en vers. La première, ce sont les différences de grammaire et de vocabulaire, qui ne permettent pas de rendre par des correspondants exacts, soit les mots, soit les tours de l'original. La seconde, c'est la nature même de la poésie, qui consiste dans un rapport de l'idée avec le vers, c'est-à-dire avec une mesure, une cadence et des sons, et qui s'altère lorsque la traduction substitue une versification à une autre . . . Ainsi notre vers n'a pas les mêmes qualités mélodiques que le vers étranger, il n'en rend pas le son, il n'en traduit pas la sensation, bref, sous ce premier et capital rapport, il ne le reproduit pas" (5, 324–5).

far appeared some, such as the Lucretius and the Homer, have been in prose, but others, such as the *Faust* and the *Inferno,* in verse. Another recent British development has been the commissioning of verse translations of certain classics for performance over the third program of the BBC. In the course of all this activity a few modern translations have begun to attain observable prestige and popularity, as though a future generation might almost be expected to place on the shelf beside Fitzgerald's *Rubáiyát* or Chapman's *Homer,* Yeats' *Oedipus King,* Mac-Neice's *Agamemnon,* or Pound's Propertius. Finally, it is scarcely surprising that, of the European classics Dryden himself translated, several have found new translators among twentieth-century poets: for example, the two recent renderings of the *Aeneid* by Rolfe Humphries (1951) and C. Day-Lewis (1952).

The activity which calls itself verse translation, then, flourishes and has long flourished; how may its nature be rationally defined?

I think it can be fairly well demonstrated that a poem which purports to translate a foreign poem will, if successful, constitute both (1) a new English poem of intrinsic interest and (2) an interpretation of the original on which it was based, or out of which it grew. It can thus have a double claim on our attention.

As an illustration, let us consider the following pair of poems. The first is by A. E. Housman:

> The snows are fled away, leaves on the shaws
>   And grasses in the mead renew their birth,
> The river to the riverbed withdraws,
>   And altered is the fashion of the earth.
>
> The Nymphs and Graces three put off their fear
>   And unapparelled in the woodland play.
> The swift hour and the brief prime of the year
>   Say to the soul, *Thou wast not born for aye.*
>
> Thaw follows frost; hard on the heel of spring
>   Treads summer sure to die, for hard on hers
> Comes autumn with his apples scattering;
>   Then back to wintertide, when nothing stirs.
>
> But oh, whate'er the sky-led seasons mar,
>   Moon upon moon rebuilds it with her beams:
> Come *we* where Tullus and where Ancus are,
>   And good Aeneas, we are dust and dreams.
>
> Torquatus, if the gods in heaven shall add
>   The morrow to the day, what tongue has told?

Feast then thy heart, for what thy heart has had
The fingers of no heir will ever hold.

When thou descendest once the shades among,
The stern assize and equal judgment o'er,
Not thy long lineage nor thy golden tongue,
No, nor thy righteousness, shall friend thee more.

Night holds Hippolytus the pure of stain,
Diana steads him nothing, he must stay;
And Theseus leaves Pirithous in the chain
The love of comrades cannot take away.[3]

The second is by Samuel Johnson:

The snow, dissolv'd, no more is seen,
The fields and woods, behold! are green;
The changing year renews the plain,
The rivers know their banks again;
The sprightly nymph and naked grace
The mazy dance together trace;
The changing year's successive plan
Proclaims mortality to man.
Rough winter's blasts to spring give way,
Spring yields to summer's sovereign ray;
Then summer sinks in autumn's reign,
And winter chills the world again;
Her losses soon the moon supplies,
But wretched man, when once he lies
Where Priam and his sons are laid,
Is nought but ashes and a shade.
Who knows if Jove, who counts our score,
Will toss us in a morning more?
What with your friend you nobly share,
At least you rescue from your heir.
Not you, Torquatus, boast of Rome,
When Minos once has fixed your doom,
Or eloquence, or splendid birth,
Or virtue, shall restore to earth.
Hippolytus, unjustly slain,
Diana calls to life in vain;
Nor can the might of Theseus rend
The chains of hell that hold his friend.

3. "Diffugere Nives," *The Collected Poems of A. E. Housman* (Henry Holt, 1940).
Also copyright 1936, Barclays Bank, Ltd.

Each poem is somewhat characteristic of its author. Obviously,

> Comes autumn with his apples scattering;
> Then back to wintertide, when nothing stirs

is not unlike the much more familiar

> And stands about the woodland ride
> Wearing white for Eastertide.

Similarly the couplet

> The changing year's successive plan
> Proclaims mortality to man

has the energetic abstraction characteristic of Johnsonian rhetoric— especially characteristic when, as here, it is flanked on either side by simpler and more concrete language. Going beyond the individual authors, one can see that the more elaborate specification of scenic effects in the first is also characteristic of the century in which it was written. These seem, however, relatively superficial differences when compared with the next I shall mention.

Each poem is about death, and the effect of death on man. According to Housman, whose phrase "dust and dreams" seems to evoke the sort of Swinburnian (illusory) afterlife dramatized in "The Garden of Proserpine," the upright character of Torquatus will become irrelevant at the moment of his death and dissolution; it will not "friend thee more." This prediction knocks the props out from under the "assize" and "judgment" mentioned earlier in the same stanza: the assize is "stern," apparently, because the prospect is gloomy; and the judgment "equal" because important culprits and paragons of virtue are going to get identical sentences. In the corresponding stanza of Johnson's, where "ashes and a shade" imply the contents of a burial urn ("ashes") as contrasted with the inhabitants of an Homeric underworld ("a shade"), Torquatus is simply informed that he will not be "restored to earth," whatever his life has formerly been like; the possibility is left open that Minos might take that life into account in fixing his postmortal doom.

Another obvious difference is the immediate advice which follows upon each poet's conception of the ultimate future for Torquatus. Housman wants him to "feast his heart" in an unspecified manner, though possibly on the recurrent beauties afforded by the changing seasons; Johnson wants him to share something (what? the amenities accruing from his substantial position in the Roman commonwealth?) nobly with a friend—presumably the speaker of the poem. This couplet of Johnson's looks forward to the separation of dead from living lovers and comrades with which the poem concludes.

But everything mentioned so far seems to me less important than the divergence in *manner* of the two poems. Here the sort of poetic diction employed in each is significant, particularly Housman's use of the archaic second person singular.

> Feast then thy heart, for what thy heart has had
> The fingers of no heir will ever hold

resembles in tone

> Remember now thy Creator in the days of thy youth, while the evil days come not, nor the years draw nigh, when thou shalt say, I have no pleasure in them

from the final chapter of Ecclesiastes. Such portentousness Johnson's

> What with your friend you nobly share,
> At least you rescue from your heir

entirely escapes. The same thing could be said of

> Torquatus, if the gods in heaven shall add
> The morrow to the day, what tongue has told?

as compared to

> Who knows if Jove, who counts our score,
> Will toss us in a morning more?

And of course the rhythmical differences markedly support the contrasts in language. Johnson's short lines trot; Housman's larger quatrains linger like a dirge or a funeral march.

When we come to the Latin—for by this time it will of course be no secret that the two poems have a common original in that tongue—I had better first quote, if only to make the point that the sound effects of neither English poem are much like those of Horace's (this ode, the seventh of the fourth book, is one of his most famous). The Latin meter is simple dactylic hexameter and trimeter:

> Diffugere nives, redeunt jam gramina campis
>   Arboribusque comae;
> Mutat terra vices, et decrescentia ripas
>   Flumina praetereunt;
>
> Gratia cum Nymphis geminisque sororibus audet
>   Ducere nuda choros.
> Immortalia ne speres, monet annus et almum
>   Quae rapit hora diem.
>
> Frigora mitescunt Zephyris, ver proterit aestas,
>   Interitura simul

Pomifer Autumnus fruges effuderit, et mox
Bruma recurrit iners.

Damna tamen celeres reparant caelestia lunae:
Nos, ubi decidimus
Quo pater Aeneas, quo Tullus dives et Ancus,
Pulvis et umbra sumus.

Quis scit an adiciant hodiernae crastina summae
Tempora di superi?
Cuncta manus avidas fugient heredis, amico
Quae dederis animo.

Cum semel occideris, et de te splendida Minos
Fecerit arbitria,
Non, Torquate, genus, non te facundia, non te
Restituet pietas.

Infernis neque enim tenebris Diana pudicum
Liberat Hippolytum
Nec Lethaea valet Theseus abrumpere caro
Vincula Perithoo.

One of the most obvious physical aspects of the Horatian ode is the steady alternate dilation and contraction of the line unit, a rhythmic change which, once it has been established as a feature of the poem, can be used to give an epigrammatic jolt to individual parts. Thus the long line about father Aeneas and the early rulers wealthy Tullus and Ancus is succeeded by the brief "Pulvis et umbra sumus"; and thus the elaborate, interrupted, protesting catalogue of Torquatus' attributes ("Non, Torquate, genus, non te facundia, non te") abruptly and decisively culminates in the two words "Restituet pietas" (and your piety isn't going to bring you back either!). The flexibility of Latin word order and the pre-established clarity of its syntax have, of course, a good deal to do with making such effects possible to Horace and impossible to his English imitators.

Any attempt to use the words of the Latin poem, taken one by one, as a sort of composite litmus paper to adjudicate the differences between Johnson's version of it and Housman's must at once run up against a series of awkward facts, two of which are compression in Johnson and expansion in Housman. What has become, in Johnson, of apple-bearing autumn scattering her fruits? Where, in Horace, is there anything about the chain of death being one "which love of comrades cannot take away"? [4] A more elaborate analysis of the three poems would in general

4. For that matter, neither English poet has been too particular about dictionary meanings: I have a Latin-English lexicon on my shelf which gives twenty-eight separate equivalents for the word *nudus*, used in Horace's second stanza to apply to the Grace who

show that Housman, as one might expect from the comparative length of his lines and the scope this gives him, has fixed his eye much more closely than Johnson has on various details in Horace; but that on one point at least, the question of just how ineffective a good life is in the afterworld, Johnson and Horace are much more clearly saying the same sort of thing than are Horace and Housman.

Talk about the dictionary, however, really implies not a comparison between an English poem and Horace's but rather a comparison between an English poem and a possible literal prose translation of Horace, which is quite another matter. The fact that Horace was not jotting down a few random musings in a letter to a friend but composing a poem means, as inspection of the result readily shows, that he was shaping something in which an elaborate organization of language—for example the long-short line alternations—concurs with a series of images and statements in a way that simply does not happen in prose. The same general sort of concurrence can, however, obviously take place in other poems; and does so, I feel, to a large extent in Housman's and to a certain extent in Johnson's.

The problem of which poem wins the contest, in whatever terms the rules are conceived, is less curious, however, than the wide and obvious differences among all three. This circumstance has a certain irony. Here are two Latinists, each among the best known his nation has ever produced and each also a competent English poet. In other words, here are two men who are about as well qualified to translate a lyric of Horace's, we would suppose, as any we are likely to find; both happen to have translated the same lyric, and that a very famous one; and compare the two results! But though neither poem can be thought of as in any sense a substitute for the Latin, a case can be made for each as a sensitive commentary on it, one commentary being, in my judgment, somewhat richer than the other, but both having value. I would go further and add that though Johnson's poem is now deservedly much less read and reprinted than his *Vanity of Human Wishes* or "Verses on the Death of Dr. Levett," Housman's strikes me as being among the best he ever wrote, quite apart from its relation to Horace.

If a verse translation is a commentary on the original poem from which it derives, it is clear, however, that it is a different kind of commentary from that which would be written by an editor, a scholar, or a critic. In brief, it interprets by enactment, not by analysis. Like its original, it also strives to be a verbal object whose value is inseparable from the particular words used.

---

leads the dance; and "unapparelled," which Housman has in *his* second stanza, is not among them. (Yet "unapparelled" of course fits well with the rest of Housman's diction: "wintertide," etc.) Johnson's "naked" of course is among them, but he could be picked up on any one of a number of other points.

Failure to appreciate this point is what chiefly invalidates Arnold's lectures on translating Homer. For, brilliant as many of the individual critical insights on Arnold's pages are, the lectures nevertheless proceed from shaky theoretical assumptions. Compare, for example, the two following passages:

> Pope composes with his eye on his style, into which he translates his object, whatever it is. That, therefore, which Homer conveys to us immediately, Pope conveys to us through a medium (1861 ed., p. 21).

> to call Nestor "the moss-trooping Nestor" is absurd, because, though Nestor may possibly have been much the same sort of a man as many a moss-trooper, he has yet come to us through a mode of representation so unlike that of Percy's Reliques, that, instead of "reappearing in the moss-trooping heroes" of these poems, he exists in our imagination as something utterly unlike them, and as belonging to another world (p. 56).

In the second passage Arnold is speaking, not of a translation, but of the original Greek. What has become, then, of "that which Homer conveys to us immediately"? If this "mode of representation" through which Nestor has come to us is not a medium, what is it? The truth is that Homer could no more help composing with his eye on his style than Pope, Chaucer, Shakespeare, or any other true poet; if he had taken his eye off it, the result would not have been poetry. And Homer's style being, of course, bound up intimately with the Greek language of his time, it cannot be transferred, as Arnold seems to think, into another language. It follows that, since style is the man himself, we cannot have another Homer, or a "reasonable facsimile thereof," in another age and country. What we can have is a re-creation, an interpretation—which will be good or bad according as the interpreter is a great or little poet, and has great or little insight.

3. False Expectations as to Translation

Beyond merely saying that a good translation will be both a poem, or piece of literature, in its own right and an interpretation of its original as well, can any valid generalizations be made about the kind of relationship it will probably have to that original? One set of answers to this question is predicated on the false expectation that a translation can somehow, to some degree, *reproduce* an original poem. Such expectations arise, I am convinced, out of misleading analogies drawn between literature and some other area of human activity; they result in elaborate, impractical, and often irrelevant prescriptions for translators; and they carry with them no criteria of success except external and artificial tests of an unworkable and intrinsically dubious sort. But so widespread have been these expectations in the past, and so apparently authoritative their formulation by various critics and scholars, that it will be well to review a few of the chief forms they have taken before discussing possible alternatives to them.

(A) EXPECTATIONS AS TO WORDS

The mechanical theory of verse translation takes a number of forms, but all have one element in common—the setting up of the original poem as a kind of target at which the translator is assumed to be shooting, and the grading or rating of his marksmanship by some quasi-mathematical, or at any rate "objective," formula easy to apply to the *parts* of the translation; for the mechanical theory customarily neglects the new poem as a *whole*.

The most available part is, of course, the words themselves.[5] Show any lover of a particular foreign poem a new, or old, translation of it, and ten to one the first thing he will do is select some phrase, or line, or stanza of the original and pounce on a verbal "ineptitude," or "inaccuracy," at the corresponding point in the translation. If the phraseology of the original is genuinely felicitous at the point chosen, almost any translation will, of course, be bound to be *either* "inaccurate" or "inept" —working in a different language, a translator has very little choice. The great weakness of the exact-verbal-meaning approach to translation of literature is its tendency to proceed from the assumed premise that the value of the original consists in the brilliance of this or that detached passage:

> Whan that Aprille with his shoures soote . . .

or

> Was du ererbt von deinen Vätern hast,
> Erwirb es, um es zu besitzen.

Or perhaps the assumption is that a congeries of such passages accounts for its value. Treatment of fragments of the translation seems to imply that the original is being also thought of as fragmentary.

A consequence of the verbal approach has been a demand—frequently from scholars, sometimes from critics—for prose translations of poetry. From the point of view of the literalists, this method has the advantage of allowing the dictionary meanings of all the words in the poem, and

5. "every attempt [at translation] which is not based upon a fine sense of the value of Latin words and on a careful attention to each word in every sentence, is built upon a rotten foundation and is doomed to failure . . . Every word should be represented somehow in the translation, except where (as sometimes in the omission of particles . . .) the omission of a word improves the English and takes nothing from the meaning." Alexander Souter, *Hints on Translation* (Macmillan, 1920), p. 7. The hints are aimed mainly, but not exclusively, at translators of prose.

to a large extent the original grammatical constructions, to be imitated; and thus in translations aimed chiefly at some utilitarian purpose (such as those of the Loeb library, for example) it is often employed. But even among critics dedicated to the most austere doctrines, there have been objections; for one thing, it is easy to see that "a prose translation, however deft its workmanship, cannot give the effect which verse produces; if it could, why do poets take the trouble to write verse?" [6] The possible dangers of a very close, literal rendering of verse have never been better dramatized than in Stephen Leacock's immortal burlesque of a typical classroom rendition of Homer, "as done by the very best professor, his spectacles glittering with the literary rapture of it":

"Then he too Ajax on the one hand leaped (or possibly jumped) into the fight wearing on the other hand, yes certainly a steel corselet (or possibly a bronze undertunic) and on his head of course, yes without doubt he had a helmet with a tossing plume taken from the mane (or possibly extracted from the tail) of some horse which once fed along the banks of the Scamander (and it sees the herd and raises its head and paws the ground) and in his hand a shield worth a hundred oxen and on his knees too especially in particular greaves made by some cunning artificer (or perhaps blacksmith) and he blows the fire and it is hot. Thus Ajax leapt (or, better, was propelled from behind), into the fight." [7]

The advantages of verse for rendering verse, on the other hand, have been admirably demonstrated by J. P. Postgate, in the following illustration:

Verse in itself is a more powerful engine than prose; it has a further range, and its impact is heavier. . . . How poor appears the Loeb translation of Juvenal:

haud facile emergunt quorum virtutibus obstat
res angusta domi,

It is no easy matter anywhere for a man to rise
when poverty stands in the way of his merits,

6. T. S. Omond, "Arnold and Homer," *English Association Essays and Studies* (Clarendon Press, 1912), p. 76. A good question. Some possible answers to it were suggested by William Ellery Leonard in the preface to his translation of *Lucretius* (Dutton, 1921), p. xi: "verse is preferable to prose [because]: (1) verse permits a wider and more apposite choice of syntactical constructions than the more conventional idioms of prose: (2) verse gives to the many repetitions of ideas, words, phrases, and clauses, which in a prose translation often seem mere jejune verbosity, their proper relevance and copiousness . . . ; (3) verse, by its very cadences, by its metrical emphases, possesses, for driving home the central meanings and for distinguishing the nicer contrasts and other relations of the ideas, an instrument scarcely available in the more pedestrian rhythms of prose."

7. *Laugh with Leacock* (Dodd, Mead, 1941), pp. 225–6.

when set by Johnson's

Slow rises worth by poverty depress'd.[8]

(B) EXPECTATIONS AS TO METERS

Next to the literal meanings of the words, the second most obvious feature of a foreign poem, or any poem, is certainly its meter; and the adherents of some forms of the mechanical theory of translation have had a good deal to say on this subject. Some classical scholars, for example, notably Professors J. P. Postgate and A. E. Housman,[9] apparently have convinced themselves that for certain Latin or Greek meters there are analogous optimum English meters into which any translation should be made. Thus if the original is in hexameters, the translation should be in blank verse; if in elegiac couplets, in pentameter couplets; and so forth. Postgate invokes mathematics in his consideration of poetic forms, and extends his arithmetic, by unimpeachable logic, to the number of lines permissible in a translation of a given Latin original. Thus if the original were a poem of 600 hexameters, then according to this theory it would be possible to predetermine (taking into account the differences between the two languages and between the length of the two lines) that the translation would consist, say, of 725 lines of blank verse; if an actual translation should turn out to have 50 lines too many or too few, that fact in itself would invalidate it.

The labor-saving consequences to criticism of such a theory are, of course, potentially immense. Thus Postgate is able to write (p. 91): "The rejection of rime for rendering of continuous verse disposes of the heroic couplet of Dryden and Pope" (one wonders why it does not also dispose of much of the original narrative poetry of Chaucer, Keats, etc.); while Housman rejects the translator Tremenheere's version of a certain elegy of Propertius (which he praises on every other ground) solely because it is in English tetrameters (p. 233).

The analogous meters prescription, however, is mild compared to the fascination which a related theory has exercised over a long series of critics, scholars, and translators alike: the notion, that is, that peculiar sanctity attaches to the *meter of the original poem*, quite apart from the particular words in which that meter, in the original poem, has been embodied.[1] Matthew Arnold is, of course, the most famous case in point;

8. Postgate, *Translation and Translations* (Bell, 1922), pp. 77–8.
9. See *ibid.*, pp. 65 ff., 74, 83, 91 f.; and Housman's review of Tremenheere's Propertius in *Classical Review, 14* (1900), 232–3.
1. "a poet's choice of meter is scarcely less personal or less important than his choice of a subject . . . The meter the poet chose is essential to his poem"—Edith Hamilton, *Three Greek Plays* (Norton, 1937), p. 147. The quotation is revealing: here the translator is evidently identifying very closely with the original poet. The meters in question are those of the choruses in Greek drama. Cf. also F. B. Gummere, "The Translations of Beowulf . . ." in *American Journal of Philology, 7* (1886), 47.

he wanted the *Iliad* done into English hexameters, and even composed a few hexameters to demonstrate the principle.[2]

But the supposition that an imitation of a foreign meter will constitute an imitation of a foreign poet's manner is a very strange one. In Homer, for example, the use of dactylic hexameter, which requires up to eleven short or unaccented syllables for every six long ones, is obviously related to the presence in Homer's Greek of numerous long, polysyllabic words, like πολύτροπον ("of many turnings") in the first line of the *Odyssey*. But H. B. Cotterill, a skillful versifier who translated the *Odyssey* into English dactylic hexameters in 1911, is again and again forced to an almost exclusive use of monosyllables and other short words. Two fairly typical lines run as follows:

All on the shore of the ocean in order they spread on the shingle
Where it is washed by the tides of the sea as they sweep to the dry land.[3]

It could be well argued that the effect of such verse is in some ways more un-Homeric, in respect to meter, than a prose translation would be.

With more modern languages, translation into the meters of the original may involve use of the rhyme schemes of the original—the two foreign authors where the problem has most frequently arisen being, I believe, Dante and Goethe. One difficulty has been quite analogous to that just discussed in connection with hexameters for an English Homer: Dante's Italian, somewhat like Chaucer's Middle English, made available to him a large number of polysyllabic feminine rhymes for which there is no equivalent in modern English; and Goethe worked within a German tradition of using what we would call doggerel verse for serious purposes.[4]

Bayard Taylor's colossal feat of ingenuity in translating *Faust* with close imitation of meters, rhymes, and even syllable count of the original German ought to stand as a horrible warning to future ages as to the esthetic disadvantages of such a practice. One result, however, was that his translation obtained widespread acceptance as a "standard" version in its own day, and is even at present constantly reprinted in anthologies and sometimes lavishly praised by Germanic philologists. This is true

2. Cf. Douglas Knight, *Pope and the Heroic Tradition* (Yale Univ. Press, 1951), p. 3, for a discussion of the difficulties with this program.
3. C. M. Bowra and T. F. Higham, *The Oxford Book of Greek Verse in Translation* (Clarendon Press, 1938), p. 83.
4. The most interesting modern metrical analogue to Dante I have seen is the meeting of poet and ghost in Eliot's "Little Gidding, II": a kind of unrhymed verse, arranged in groups of three lines, with masculine and feminine endings alternating in each line—a scene which has recently been called "Mr. Eliot's finest sustained passage of poetic writing . . . unequalled by any other modern poet except Yeats" (Kenneth Allott, *Penguin Book of Contemporary Verse* [1950], p. 83). So far as I know, no one has tried this method for a translation of Dante. Dorothy Sayers and Laurence Binyon are the most recent terza-rima translators of the *Divine Comedy*.

despite the fact that as long ago as 1908 a doctoral dissertation was published which snipes expertly at Taylor's theory of translation and unearths damning examples of his incompetence to put the theory effectively into practice.[5] It is possible that Taylor may fall somewhat short of the obscurity of Browning in his translation, on similar principles, of the *Agamemnon,* a version of which some one said that he "could just make it out with the aid of the original Greek"; but Taylor's *Faust* does convincingly demonstrate a basic weakness of the bold mechanical theory as applied to rhyme.

Consider the following passage in the German; here Faust is himself embarked on a translation, the original being the first sentence in the Gospel according to Saint John; he is seeking a German word for the "logos" of the original Greek:

> Geschrieben steht: "Im Anfang war das Wort!"
> Hier stock ich schon! Wer hilft mir weiter fort?
> Ich kann das *Wort* so hoch unmöglich schätzen,
> Ich muss es anders übersetzen,
> Wenn ich vom Geiste recht erleuchtet bin
> Geschrieben steht: Im Anfang war der *Sinn.*
> Bedenke wohl die erste Zeile,
> Dass deine Feder sich nicht übereile!
> Ist es der *Sinn,* der alles wirkt und schafft?
> Es sollte stehn: Im Anfang war die *Kraft!*
> Doch, auch indem ich dieses niederschreibe,
> Schon warnt mich was, dass ich dabei nicht bleibe.
> Mir hilft der Geist, auf einmal seh ich Rat
> Und schreibe getrost: Im Anfang war die *Tat!*

One of the crucial functions of rhyme in this passage is to emphasize the translator's possible choices: each alternate reading for "logos" comes at the end of a line (the most emphatic position possible) and as the second of a pair of rhyme words. In one case, indeed (schafft—Kraft: "create"—"power") the similarity of sound underlines a relationship in meaning between the rhyming words: it would take *power* to *create* anything.

Taylor's version—a fairly characteristic example of both his weaknesses and his ingenuity—runs as follows:

> 'Tis written: "In the Beginning was the *Word.*"
> Here I am balked: who, now, can help afford?
> The *Word?*—impossible so high to rate it,
> And otherwise I must translate it,

5. Juliana Haskell, *Bayard Taylor's Translation of Goethe's Faust* (Columbia Univ. Press, 1908).

If by the spirit I am truly taught.
Then thus: "In the beginning was the *Thought*."
This first line let me weigh completely,
Lest my impatient pen proceed too fleetly.
Is it the thought which works, creates, indeed?
"In the beginning was the *Power*," I read.
Yet, as I write, a warning is suggested,
That I the sense may not have fairly tested.
The spirit aids me: now I see the light!
"In the beginning was the *Act*," I write.

The first two versions of "logos," *word* and *thought* are emphasized, as in Goethe's German, by being made rhyme words; but in the second half of the passage, a strange transformation occurs. The emphasis is now, to judge from the rhymes, on the *actions* of the translating Faust rather than on his versions of the document before him: "indeed . . . I read . . . I see the light . . . I write." This of course changes the semantic shape of the passage in a way that even a literalist might be expected to find untrue to the German; and, more important from the point of view of the English poem, softens any possible climactic force.[6]

(c) EXPECTATIONS AS TO DICTION

A third salient feature of foreign literature which theorists of translation sometimes feel should be imitated is any obvious connotative effect of language—for example, an archaism or a dialectal expression. T. F. Higham's on the whole intelligent and interesting introduction to *The Oxford Book of Greek Verse in Translation* contains, none the less, some ferocious pieces of advice to aspiring verse translators: for example, that if a passage in Aeschylus parodies a passage in Euripides "there is no option for a translator but to parody the best-known English versions of Euripides" (p. 734). At another point Higham remarks: "Before a colouring of archaism is applied, two points must be settled. First, whether old words were vivid in the Greek, or dulled by long poetic usage; and second, whether a poet's innovations were not, on the whole, more important than his archaisms. The archaizing translator may then proceed, mixing his colours in a rough proportion . . ." (p. lxxx).

The phrase "a colouring of archaism is applied" tends to give away the terms in which translation is being visualized.

On the question of dialects a translation theorist named Karl Wm.

6. The passage is also characteristic in its inversions ("who can help afford," etc.); in the ambiguous "otherwise," which at first glance looks as though it might mean "under other circumstances"; and in the use of the puny expletive "indeed" as a rhyme word in the first place.

Henry Scholz has equally stringent notions.[7] He recommends that local German dialects when used in modern drama be translated by means of American analogues: "For example, . . . the Silesian peasant dialect could be rendered by the characteristic language of the Yankee farmer in any outlying country district" (p. 37). Scholz also believes that "the real cosmopolitan value of a translation can be realized only by retaining the original setting. By doing so one people is made familiar with the manners and customs of another, as well as with the *milieu* in which these people think and move" (p. 51).

All this conjures up a rather exotic mental picture. To present a Silesian peasant on the streets of a Silesian village talking in the characteristic idiom of a down-east New England farmer, or one of Joseph C. Lincoln's salty Cape Codders, will give a startlingly cosmopolitan effect, certainly; whether it will not also distract from whatever is the point of the drama itself is another question. Something like Scholz's method has, however, been tried—but not, I think, with notable success —by the translator of Thomas Mann's *Buddenbrooks*.

(D) CAUSES OF SUCH EXPECTATIONS

Let us imagine the predicament, for a moment, of a translator faced with some elaborate foreign poem, hounded by scholars quick to detect the slightest "infidelity" to the august original, and dedicated to satisfying the various expectations just described. He is familiar with the dictionary meaning of every word he must translate; he has marked in colored ink every literary device or feature—rhyme scheme, alliteration, assonances, meter, dialectal variants—of the original. He has a *Roget's Thesaurus* at his elbow, and a Walker's rhyming dictionary on his desk. What does he resemble? Obviously nothing so much as a man doing a Chinese puzzle, only with pieces that will not quite fit.[8] Why has he embarked on such a venture in the first place?

The answer is, of course, because the belief has long existed, and to some extent still exists today, that the impossible is possible: that a work of imaginative literature can somehow be "reproduced," or nearly reproduced, in another tongue.

The virulence with which this belief has sometimes been enunciated will hardly be believed without demonstration. "No painter," writes H. C. Tolman, in his *Art of Translating*, "however skillful, can reproduce a landscape *perfectly* true to nature. The best painter is . . . he who . . . paints the scene *most true* to nature. So the best translator is

7. *The Art of Translation* . . . (Univ. of Pennsylvania, 1918).
8. "La traduction ressemble toujours au casse-tête chinois, avec cette différence que, dans le jeu chinois, les pièces sont faites pour convenir à la figure géométrique dans laquelle il s'agit de les renfermer, de sorte qu'on finit toujours par y arriver, tandis que, dans la traduction en vers, on est sûr d'avance que l'adaptation laissera à désirer." Edmond Scherer, *Études sur la littérature contemporaine*, pp. 333 ff.

not he who *exactly* reproduces the original in English—for that is impossible—but he who most nearly reproduces it." [9]

But the painting analogy—which might surprise Matisse or Picasso —is less characteristic of our age, in a way, than the analogy to science:

The original designates the limit which translations, as variables, may approach, but never reach. It is a universally accepted mathematical truth that the difference between a variable and its limit can be made infinitely small. So also a translation may be made an almost perfect reproduction of the original. Again, mathematics has established the fact that a variable cannot pass beyond its limit, and so we may make the logical inference that a translation, as such, cannot be superior to its original.[1]

Such has been, and is, the mechanical theory of translation, a demonstrably false theory, but a seductive one. The results have not always been wholly satisfactory to critics. "We find little to remind us agreeably of a friend in a photograph of his corpse," commented a nineteenth-century scholar on Newman's version of Horace; [2] "If he thought the original was like that, what can he have seen in it to make him think that it was worth translating?" asked a certain Professor Sylvester concerning another luckless versifier.[3] A recent French critic notes that although certain nineteenth-century translations of Homer have been more exact than their predecessors, truer to every epithet and formula of the great original, they have nevertheless managed to give the impression that Homer is hardly literature at all: ". . . elles appartiennent à l'histoire de la philologie plutôt qu'à l'histoire de la littérature." [4]

(E) FALSE CRITERIA OF SUCCESS

I cannot leave the mechanical theory without at least mentioning an alternative, or correlative, doctrine which has, logically enough, accompanied its rise to orthodoxy among a wide group of scholars and critics:

9. (Boston, Sanborn, 1901), p. 41.
1. Scholz, *Art of Translation,* p. 4. E. S. Bates calls the view that "no translation can equal its original" a "will-o'-the-wisp axiom" and asks "where the translator has . . . an improved medium at his command, why not better results?" citing several examples (*Modern Translation,* pp. 111–12). Jowett considered that modern languages had become "more perspicuous than ancient" and felt that a translation of Plato should therefore be more precise and clear than the Greek. "Whereas in Plato we are not always certain where a sentence begins or ends; and paragraphs are few and far between . . . in the translation the balance of sentences and the introduction of paragraphs at suitable intervals must not be neglected if the harmony of the English language is to be preserved" (preface, 1892, p. xviii).
2. John Conington, *Quarterly Review, 104* (1858), 351. Cf. Hugh Kenner, "Hellas without Helicon," *Poetry, 84* (1954), 112–18.
3. Cf. Bridges, *Ibant Obscuri,* p. 140.
4. P. E. Mazon, *Madame Dacier et les traducteurs d'Homère* (1936), p. 21.

this is the belief that a translation can be appropriately tested, like a medicine, by observing the patient's reactions—provided, of course, that you select the right patient. Here are a few quotations which at once set forth the belief itself and trace it back to its probable originator (or at any rate to its chief exponent) :

1922 : A widely accepted definition [of the "truth" of a translation] is "the reproduction in the translation of the impression produced by the original." Who is to be the judge whether these impressions are similar? . . . In a word the Expert, not the General Reader.

1909 : *The aim of a translation should be to produce an impression similar, or as nearly as may be similar, to that produced by the original.* This is the first and fundamental proposition. To it is sometimes added a further appendage, more especially in the case of the ancient classics; namely, *an impression similar to that produced by the original on its original hearers or readers.*

1901 : . . . translation is arousing in the English reader or hearer the identical emotions and sentiments that were aroused in him who read the sentence as his native tongue.

1891 : Die neuen Verse sollen auf ihre Leser dieselbe Wirkung tun wie die alten zu ihrer Zeit auf ihr Volk und heute noch auf die, welche sich die nötige Mühe philologischer Arbeit gegeben haben.

1861 : Let him [the translator] ask how his work affects those who both know Greek and can appreciate poetry; whether to read it gives the Provost of Eton, or Professor Thompson at Cambridge, or Professor Jowett here in Oxford, at all the same feeling which to read the original gives them . . . He is trying to satisfy scholars, because scholars alone have the means of really judging him.[5]

But if the mechanical theory itself is difficult to apply in practice, testing the effect of the original or the translation by appeal to experts will be, if anything, more difficult. What classicist will have the temerity to describe the "effect" of the Homeric poems on their original hearers, when it is still a matter of dispute in what century the poems first appeared, or who those hearers were? Who will trust the esthetic judgment of a Richard Bentley concerning the *Iliad* when the effect on him of *Paradise Lost* is so widely and scandalously known? On all counts it seems inevitable that for literature in general and poetry in particular the notion of replicas, whether in terms of details of the original or in terms of "emotions," "sentiments," or other effects in the minds of a

5. 1922 : Postgate, *Translation and Translations,* p. 19; 1909: T. H. Warren, *Essays of Poets and Poetry,* pp. 103–4; 1901: Tolman, *The Art of Translating,* p. 22; 1891: U. Wilamowitz-Moellendorff, *Euripides Hippolytos, Griechisch und Deutsch* (Berlin, Weidmannsche Buchh., 1891), p. 6; M. Arnold, *On Translating Homer,* pp. 4, 30.

specialized group of readers, must be abandoned at the outset; and an attempt must be made to formulate, however tentatively, some sort of alternative.

4. *A Theory of Translation*

A work of literature appears to be a system of symbols; to such an extent is this true that in the greatest poetry even details of meter, etc., often have symbolic force. To take a single line as an example, when Milton has the Son create the universe out of chaos, the initial order is given:

> "Silence, ye troubled waves; and thou deep, peace."
> (*Paradise Lost*, VII, 216)

Change the word order slightly, and the power of the line decreases; thus in Bentley's emendation, quoted by William Empson in *Some Versions of Pastoral,*

> "Silence, ye troubled waves, and peace, thou deep"

"peace," no longer being at the end of the line, loses its climactic emphasis and part of its parallelism to "Silence"; the meter is weaker and more regular because the final foot, an interrupted spondee in "deep, peace" has become a regular iambic in "thou deep"; the contrast in meaning between an oceanic chaos and a divine harmony is less insistent when the two words "peace" and "deep" have been separated by an unaccented expletive; the two long-e sounds now no longer come in adjacent syllables, and the two p's (of "deep" and "peace") no longer have to be pronounced one on top of the other—verbal effects which, in the line as we read it today, simultaneously produce an illusion of echo and push the two words apart, reinforcing the basic contrast in idea.

It is also true, however, that the total context of the line—that is, the epic *Paradise Lost*—is important in giving the slight semantic details their symbolic weight. If we could imagine the command being given by an oratorical sea captain, in a poem imitative of Masefield, at the moment when oil is about to be poured from the deck of a freighter in a hurricane, then the revision "peace, thou deep" might actually be preferable; for then the final word "deep" would direct attention *away* from the result and the speaker, and toward the ocean, which might or might not be about to respond. In Milton, any suggestion that command and obedience are not simultaneous—indeed, almost synonymous—could hardly help weakening the concept of deity (and of the cosmos) about which the whole poem centers.

I would call this concept of deity one of the pillar symbols of *Paradise Lost;* others are the actors in the narrative (Adam, Satan, and the rest) ; the sequence of events; the picture of a universal order, often called the great chain of being, contrasted with the differing sorts of disorder described in hell and earth after the fall; and the general ideological, or theological, bases of the poem, set forth chiefly in Book III. Such pillar symbols, though of course the poem presents them entirely in words (literature has no other option), can be thought of separately, I suggest, from symbolic details such as the meter and word order of the "Silence, ye troubled waves" line which have just been described. They are never *experienced* separately from the words that embody them; but after the poem has been set aside and the lines (except for isolated bits or short passages, like the one quoted) are no longer in mind, they may still be *remembered* separately, so that an account of them could be communicated to someone who had never read the poem.

A second point about literary symbols is that, in successful works, a reader cannot be indifferent to them. Admirers of *Paradise Lost* even today still quarrel about the "heroism" or "contemptibility" of Satan; but no competent reader fails to have some sort of reaction to him. Poetic symbols embody *attitudes*—toward themselves and toward other symbols of the works in which they appear.

Under the term pillar symbol—that is, a symbol of basic structural importance to an imaginative work—I include not only the ideologies, such as that of *Paradise Lost,* but also any logical sequence of ideas, or any sequence of images. The earth spirit tells the professor in Goethe's *Faust,* that "you resemble the spirit which you can grasp, not me" (*Du gleichst dem Geist, den du begreifst, Nicht mir!*) ; then disappears, leaving Faust alone in his study. "Whom do I resemble then?" asks the despairing Faust; there is immediately a knock at the door, and the pedant Wagner, embodiment of all that Faust is trying to escape, enters. The play is full of such transitions, sudden and ironic.

Prose fiction of a traditional sort ordinarily is composed of a dense texture of pillar symbols: narrative, reflections or philosophy, exposition. (I call the more abstract parts of literature symbols because of their initial relevance to the surrounding symbolism of the works in which they occur: "Beauty is truth, truth beauty" has first of all something to do with the urn.) Much modern poetry, and some modern fiction, makes use of seemingly arbitrary symbol sequences, counterfeiting a resemblance to the free associations of daydreams.

In poetry as opposed to prose, a recurrent alogical interrupter, the ending of each line, is introduced into discourse as a complicating factor: there is no reason in the logic of the sentence itself why "Whether 'tis nobler in the mind to suffer the slings and arrows of outrageous fortune" should break after "suffer" and before "the slings," though ordinarily in a great deal of poetry (that of Marianne Moore is a noteworthy exception), logic and line ending will often be made to coincide

("To be or not to be; that is the question"). The presence of the recurrent interruptions serves to divert attention to other alogical elements of poetic statement. When lines are metrically similar, we are made aware of the rise and fall of accent (no one, in reading a novel aloud, hesitates about which word or syllable to stress in a given sequence—stress, except for the demands of logic, is unimportant); and anyone aware of the rise and fall of accent becomes also aware of other physical contours in language—alliteration, assonance, etc. Rhyme and stanzaic forms are further complicating, alogical factors, having similar effects to the presence of the line itself. The arbitrary physical shape of poetry makes for the constant potentiality of *local* symbolism—as opposed to pillar symbolism—of the sort involved in "Silence, ye troubled waves, and thou deep, peace." Local symbolism can be very important in the creation of attitude: in T. S. Eliot's "The Hollow Men," the rhythms of the nursery rhyme "Here we go round the mulberry bush," and the fact that this particular nursery rhyme is recalled by the conclusion of the poem, have a great deal to do with stiffening and justifying the attitudes evoked in the poem as a whole and especially in the concluding word "whimper."

What the translator of a poem can do, ideally, is to construct fairly convincing analogies for pillar symbols; local symbolism he must create for himself. If he translates into prose, he either by-passes local symbolism entirely or reduces its relative effect and importance in his version. If he translates into verse with his eye firmly fixed on the mechanical, rather than the organic, aspects of the local symbolism in the original, he produces a structure in which the local symbols, instead of reflecting the pillars, are always tending to undermine them or distract attention from them. Thus in Bayard Taylor's couplet:

> Is it the thought which works, creates, indeed?
> "In the beginning was the *Power*," I read.

the rhyme element in the word "indeed" sets up a structure of local symbolism which is not only alogical but also nonfunctional—that is, perverse, chaotic. As such, it distracts from the pillar symbols operating in the passage, the series of fresh assaults on the Greek text by the mind of Faust. In the German, as we have seen, there had been a very precise fusion of local and pillar symbols at this point, in the *schafft-Kraft* rhymes. Concentration on the physical divorced from the semantic elements in the passage has misled the indefatigable translator; and his whole version of *Faust* is always going astray in just this manner.

Local symbolism ordinarily works subconsciously, except in these analytical days when we as critics are continually fishing the subconscious up from beneath the surface of each reading and inspecting it in the light of our theories. The greatest temptation of the translator of poetry resides in the illusion that the subconscious effects of local symbolism will somehow attach themselves to *any* faithful transcription of the pillar symbols. Gilbert Murray has a famous passage on the subject, taking as an example the seventeenth-century hack translator Creech:

> a translator cannot help seeing his own work through the medium of that greater thing which he studies and loves. The light of the original shines through it, and the music of the original echoes round it. Creech's versions of Horace and Theocritus . . . may be to us unreadable; bad verse in themselves, and full of Creech's tiresome personality, the Horace no Horace of ours, and the Theocritus utterly unlike Theocritus. But to Creech himself, how different it all was! He did not know how bad his lines were. He did not feel any veil of intervening Creech. To him the Theocritus was not Creech, but pure Theocritus, or, if not quite that, at least something haunted by all the magic of Theocritus. When he read his baldest lines his voice, no doubt, trembled with emotion. . . . The original was always there present to him in a kind of symbol, its beauty perhaps even increased by that idealisation and endearment which naturally attend the long and loving service of one human mind to another.[6]

"Veil of intervening Creech." The "veil" is the local symbolism, the nub of any translator's problem.

In his original, of course, he will normally find the closest linkage between the pillar symbols, which he can do something toward translating, and the local symbols, which will ordinarily elude his grasp. The most capable translator will solve this problem by the creation of new local symbolism which will reflect, as closely as possible, his understanding of the analogies in his own work to the pillar-symbols of the original. But the analogies cannot remain unaffected by the new local symbols, and hence will suffer at least some displacement of meaning relative to the original, if the new poem is in the least alive. Pope, for example, manipulates the language of Homer's recurrent prayers to the gods, and that of other religious symbolism in Homer; but this manipulation affects the pillar symbols of the new poem, the gods themselves; and the concept of deity in Pope's *Iliad* is closer, in consequence, to that of Milton or Virgil than it is to that of the original Greek.[7] The concept of deity affects the concept of destiny, and hence the meaning of what the human actors in the *Iliad* do, and hence the central theme of the poem.

Good translators, then, will begin by grasping firmly the pillar symbols of the original poem and forming some consistent concept of how

6. Murray, *Euripides Translated into English Rhyming Verse* (George Allen, 1902), pp. x–xi.
7. Cf. Douglas Knight, *Pope and the Heroic Tradition*, pp. 50–3, 96–8.

they should be interpreted; for only on the basis of such a concept can convincing local symbols ever be created. Housman sees Horace's "Pulvis et umbra" ode as a melancholy lament, and translates it into pentameter quatrains; Johnson sees it as gaily hedonistic, and uses octosyllabic couplets—the meter of *Hudibras* and "To His Coy Mistress." Robert Bridges, a translator so obsessed by a quixotic concern for fidelity to local symbolism that he worked out a complex scheme of versification to "reproduce" in English what he thought were the exact effects of classical hexameter, nevertheless used, in one line of his rendering of Virgil, the phrase "That bright sprigg of weird" to designate the golden bough which gained Aeneas entrance to the underworld.[8] By such language he brought all the connotations of Norse mythology into his English *Aeneid*.

Such examples are extreme and dramatic, perhaps; in the translation of prose fiction the effects produced by the new local symbolism will of course be subtler, and the range of variation no doubt much less.[9] But dramatic examples ought to serve as a warning to writers on translation.

As a theorist of translation Dryden, who wrote well on this subject in the prefaces of his *Ovid's Epistles* (1680) and *Sylvae* (1685), had the advantage of living before the nineteenth century, when, as a recent student of translation theory puts it: "The rise of a more exact scholarship, the growing interest in the past for its own sake and in other literatures for their unique gusto, slowly changed the ideal of English translation . . . the growing demand of Romanticism that Celtic literature be as Celtic as possible, and Hottentot literature as Hottentot, in order that the thrill of novelty might be maintained, drove translators . . . to more and more minute fidelity."[1]

In general, as is well known, Dryden distinguished three sorts of translation: metaphrase, or word-for-word, line-for-line renderings; paraphrase, his own method, "where the author is kept in view by the translator, so as never to be lost, but his words are not so strictly followed as his sense; and that too is admitted to be amplified, but not altered";[2] and imitation, which he describes in terms that would apply as accurately to Pope's Horace or Johnson's Juvenal as to the seventeenth-

---

8. *Ibant Obscuri*, p. 39, l. 409.

9. But we are much closer, culturally speaking, to modern novels than to many great poems. Ancient prose fiction can confront the translator with considerable options and problems; Robert Graves' *Golden Ass* caused controversy on account of the translator's "style."

1. J. W. Draper, "The Theory of Translation in the Eighteenth Century," *Neophilologus*, 6 (1921), p. 254. Cf. J. S. Phillimore, *Some Remarks on Translation and Translators* (Oxford Univ. Press, 1919), p. 19: "Browning's position [in favor of literalness 'at every cost save that of absolute violence to our language'] is distinctively modern; such a claim would be inconceivable earlier than the nineteenth century. Call it, if you like, one of the many significant symptoms of the anarchy of thought and art which marked that century."

2. *Essays,* ed. W. P. Ker (Clarendon Press, 1900), *1, 237.*

century examples he cites. The principal effects of his paraphrase theory are to make clear to the public, in a general way, what sort of relation his new poems would bear to their originals; and to leave himself a fairly free hand in the construction of these new poems. We must now consider his results.

III

Dryden's Methods: Local Effects

1. *Words*

T HE WORDS,'' Dryden wrote of his translations from Chaucer, "are given up as a post not to be defended in our poet";[1] and although he was here referring to the changes the English language itself had undergone in the course of three centuries (Chaucer "wanted the modern art of fortifying"), the flexibility he practiced (like that of any Renaissance translator) upon the literal prose sense of *The Canterbury Tales,* is not essentially different from his methods with other, foreign poets. The easiest and commonest way of classifying such methods is under the rubrics compression, expansion, and substitution—that is, substitution of a new statement for what the foreign poet had, literally, said.

Thus Chaucer's ten words about a statue of Diana, "undernethe hir feet she hadde a moone, Wexynge it was" ("The Knight's Tale," 2077–8), shrink to five in Dryden—"She trod a wexing moon" ("Palamon and Arcite," II, 649). On the other hand, the four words that complete the same couplet in the original, "and sholde wanye soone," give place to eleven in Dryden's couplet, with an expansion of the thought:

> She trod a wexing moon, that soon would wane,
> And, drinking borrow'd light, be fill'd again.

When Theseus the heroic king transmits his decisions to an audience in the same poem, Chaucer has them announced by a couplet:

> An heraud on a scaffold made an "Oo!"
> Til al the noyse of peple was ydo . . ."
> (2533–4)

Dryden, by a phrase:

> Silence is thrice enjoin'd . . .
> (III, 496)

On the other hand, Virgil's half line, in the description of Hades, "sacrae panduntur portae"[2] (the sacred gates lie open), becomes a full line in the translation: "Then, of itself, unfolds th'eternal door."

---

1. *Essays,* ed. Ker, 2, 256.
2. Half line in length: actually the words are divided between two lines (*Aeneid,* VI, 573–4) ; cf. Dryden, VI, 774.

More drastic are those expansions in which Dryden supplies a line, or more than a line, embodying images or ideas clearly of his own creation. In the following vignette from the eighth book of the *Aeneid*, the last line quoted has its basis not in the Latin but in the scene itself:

> The time when early housewives leave the bed;
> When living embers on the hearth they spread,
> Supply the lamp, and call the maids to rise—
> With yawning mouths, and with half-open'd eyes . . .
>
> (VIII, 541–4)

Similarly, to Chaucer's description of the widow's bower and hall at the opening of "The Nun's Priest's Tale" (three cows, a sheep called Malle, etc.), Dryden adds a parlor window stuck with herbs, a carpet of rushes, and a maple dresser; moreover he makes the cows brindled, and Malle a ewe.

Substitution, the third process, is not essentially different from compression or expansion; indeed the theory discussed in Chapter II would suggest its inevitability in all translation of poetry, since close or exact equivalents of few foreign expressions can ordinarily be found. There are cases, however, where no equivalent, not even an approximate one, occurs in Dryden as compared with his original; and where, at the same time, something else has taken the place of what is gone. Virgil's Dido appeals to the goddess Hecate thus:

> nocturnisque Hecate triviis ululata per urbes
>
> (IV, 609)

Dryden's, thus:

> Thou Hecate hearken from thy dark abodes!
>
> (IV, 874)

Here the dark abodes (Hecate was queen of the underworld, among other things) replace what Fairclough, in the Loeb Virgil, renders as follows: "[Hecate] whose name is shrieked by night at the crossroads of cities." In "The Wife of Bath's Tale," to give a second example, Chaucer describes the hero's initial act of violence in these words: "By verray force, he rafte hire maydenhed" (888); here Dryden's "By force accomplish'd his obscene desire" simultaneously eliminates mention of the victim's innocence and puts a judgment upon the rape into the narrator's mouth.

The preceding examples will be misleading if they suggest that the degree of Dryden's latitude with the prose sense of an original is always a simple matter to determine (let alone evaluate) in any particular case. The kinds of complexity involved can be graphically illustrated in connection with perhaps the most widely quoted single line of Virgil's

Aeneid: "Sunt lacrimae rerum et mentem mortalia tangunt," the line whose prose sense, as the nineteenth century understood it, undoubtedly inspired part of the last stanza of Wordsworth's "Laodamia":

> Yet tears to human suffering are due;
> And mortal hopes defeated and o'erthrown
> Are mourned by man, and not by man alone
> As fondly he believes.

The reader who turns to the relevant passage of Dryden's *Aeneid* to look for the now famous elegiac generalization will at first suppose that it has disappeared entirely. Aeneas and his follower Achates, shipwrecked near Carthage in their voyage from ruined Troy, have entered the foreign city incognito and are surprised to find depicted, on the walls of a newly built temple, scenes from the very battles around Troy which they themselves once took part in. Aeneas, in Dryden, addresses Achates:

> O friend! ev'n here
> The monuments of Trojan woes appear!
> Our known disasters fill ev'n foreign lands:
> See there, where old unhappy Priam stands!
> Ev'n the mute walls relate the warrior's fame,
> And Trojan griefs the Tyrians' pity claim.
>
> (I, 644–9)

This last line—"And Trojan griefs the Tyrians' pity claim"—is the nearest the passage apparently comes to Virgil's "There are tears for things, and mortal matters touch the heart."

But the distance between the literal sense of Latin and English here is, according to a recent scholar, mostly apparent; it rests on a popular misunderstanding of Virgil's "sunt." This verb ("there are") is here repeated from the preceding line; the two lines together run:

> En Priamus. Sunt hic etiam sua praemia laudi;
> Sunt lacrimae rerum et mentem mortalia tangunt . . .
>
> (I, 461–2)

And since the force of "hic etiam," which follows the first "sunt," is to be also understood as affecting the second, a literal version of the second should begin "there are, even here [in Africa] . . ."

That is to say, Aeneas, far from home and unsure of his safety in an unfamiliar city, is relieved to find that *even here,* in Carthage, there is praise and pity. "Aeneas is not concerned with 'universal tears,' but with the particular prospect of a hostile reception," says R. H. Martin in his comment on the passage;[3] and Martin also remarks that although "Dry-

3. R. H. Martin, "Note on Dryden's *Aeneid*," *Philological Quarterly, 30* (1951), 89–91.

den's antithesis of Trojan griefs and Tyrians' pity is more in the pointed
style of Ovid and Dryden himself, it is nevertheless implicit in the Latin
—'even here (in Africa) we (Trojans) may hope for pity.' "

The passage illustrates how, before the effect of a given substitution
can be assessed, before even the extent to which one sense has really re-
placed another can be determined, an analysis may have to be made not
only of single words or phrases but of the entire passage—perhaps even
of the entire poem—in which the replacement occurs.

The passage also illustrates the inadequacy of the compression-
expansion-substitution formula for dealing with Dryden's changes of
the literal sense; for here he has compressed Virgil's orotund statement
about grief to the single word "pity"; but he has also expanded the
thought by means of the precise terms "Trojan" and "Tyrians' "; and
these changes amount to a substitution. The image of compression and
expansion is unfortunate, too, in its suggestion that part of a poet's
meaning is a kind of gaseous matter subject to an indeterminate Boyle's
law under the pressures of a translator's unhappy necessities. I would
prefer, therefore, to consider some examples of Dryden's manipulations
of literal meaning as they are influenced by his general inheritance from
the past, by his awareness of the needs of literature during his lifetime,
and by his sensitivity to "meanings" beyond the literal meaning of the
words in a foreign poem.

Anyone who compared the description of Arcite's funeral in Dryden's "Palamon and Arcite" with the passage on which it is based in
Chaucer's "Knight's Tale" would at once be struck by the translator's
radical rehandling of the list of trees cut down to serve the hero's funeral
pyre. Chaucer names them in the following manner:

> But how the fyr was maked upon highte,
> Ne eek the names that the trees highte,
> As ook, firre, birch, aspe, alder, holm, popler,
> Wylugh, elm, plane, assh, box, chasteyn, lynde, laurer,
> Mapul, thorn, bech, hasel, ew, whippeltree,—
> How they weren feld, shal not be toold for me; . . .
> (2919–24)

Dryden drastically reduces the size of the forest, and adds attributes to
its constituent parts, as follows:

> the trees were unctuous fir,
> And mountain-ash, the mother of the spear;
> The mourner yew and builder oak were there;
> The beech, the swimming alder, and the plane,
> Hard box, and linden of a softer grain,

And laurels, which the gods for conqu'ring
    chiefs ordain.

(III, 959–64)

The translation is a signal instance of how what I have called pillar
symbols—central images—may be preserved at the same time that the
attitudes communicated by them are shifted; for Chaucer's intention here
is partly humorous, Dryden's not. This aspect of the passages demands
to be considered in the light of the two poems—original and translation
—as complete entities;[4] but another aspect is the presence of a long
poetic tradition, within the context of which Dryden is here translating.
The catalogue of trees, as a literary device, extends through Renaissance
and Middle Ages back to antiquity, appearing in the works of at least
sixteen writers including Drayton, William Browne, Sidney, Tasso,
Boccaccio, Statius, Ovid, Virgil, and Ennius.[5] Dryden's manner in this
passage, moreover, is like that of Chaucer in another poem,[6] and very
much like that of Spenser, near the opening of *The Faerie Queene* (I,
Canto i, 8–9) :

> Much can they praise the trees so straight and hy,
> The sayling pine, the cedar proud and tall,
> The vine-prop elme, the poplar never dry,
> The builder oake, sole king of forests all,
> The aspine good for staves, and cypresse funerall,
>
> The laurel, meed of mightie conquerours,
> And poets sage, the firre that weepeth still,
> The willow worne of forlorne paramours,
> The eugh obedient to the benders will,
> The birch for shaftes, the sallow for the mill,
> The mirrhe sweete bleeding in the bitter wound,
> The warlike beech, the ash for nothing ill,
> The fruitfull olive, and the plantane round,
> The carver holme, the maple seeldom inward sound.[7]

The emotional force of such writing, the force which keeps such an in-
herited convention alive, comes, I should say, from its various and complex linkage of man's nonhuman surroundings with perennial human
purposes and concerns : one looks at a forest and sees a civilization im-

---

4. See below, Ch. iv, p. 80.
5. See Douglas Bush, *Mythology and the Renaissance Tradition in English Poetry*
(Univ. of Minnesota Press, 1932), p. 161 n.
6. See the *Parlement of Foules,* ll. 176–82, where a "builder oak" also occurs.
7. Spenserian influence in Dryden's *Fables,* though not, I think, in connection with this
passage, has been pointed out before; see Van Doren, *Poetry of Dryden,* p. 227; also Leigh
Hunt, *Men, Women and Books* (1847), *1,* 234–5.

plicit in each branch, each trunk. What has happened in the translation at this point is that the pressure of the tradition within which Chaucer wrote is apparently greater on Dryden than is the exact literal meaning of Chaucer's phrases in the catalogue. There has thus occurred an adjustment of tone, which can only be evaluated in terms of Dryden's "Palamon and Arcite" as a whole.

Elsewhere in the same poem Dryden translates Arcite's cry of woe " 'Allas,' quod he, 'that day that I was bore!' " (1542) as follows:

> Curst be the day when first I did appear;
> Let it be blotted from the calendar,
> Lest it pollute the months, and poison all
>   the year.
>
> (II, 89–91)

He is thinking of Job's blasphemous curse: "Let the day perish wherein I was born . . . let it not be joined unto the days of the year, let it not come into the number of the months . . . let them curse it that curse the day, who are ready to raise up their mourning" (III, 3 ff.)—an allusion which of course affects the figure of Arcite in the translation.[8] In yet another passage, the appeal of the widowed queens to Theseus, Dryden has their spokesman condemn an atrocity practiced upon their fallen husbands in these lines:

> But Creon, old and impious, who commands
> The Theban city, and usurps the lands,
> Denies the rites of fun'ral fires to those
> Whose breathless bodies yet he calls his foes.
>
> (I, 81–8)

The principal novelty of the translation is the last line quoted, which extends and intensifies a moral judgment already implicit in the Chaucerian original. "Whose breathless bodies yet he calls his foes," which sounds like satire, actually embodies with great precision the attitude taken by the Creon of Sophocles' *Antigone*—indeed the attitude about the rightness or wrongness of which that whole play revolves. The roots of Dryden's translations extend, sometimes, far back into the past.

Very much in the present, however, is Dryden's keen pervasive sense of his obligation to the immediate public who would purchase and explore his modern representations of distant, ancient, or unfamiliar authors; nothing is more important in understanding many of his deviations from dictionary sense than his own position as the creator, in poetry, of the Augustan sensibility.

In the language of his Chaucerian versions, for example, Dryden makes no compromise with Middle English idiom—unlike some more

8. See below, Ch. iv, pp. 74–5.

recent translations, his do not run along for a few lines in seemingly modern grammar, diction, and idiom, only to lapse abruptly into such a creaking archaism or stiff inversion as "And when you me reproach for poverty," which I quote from a widely circulated modernization of the 1930's.[9] The desire of the nineteenth century that translations of Icelandic literature be as Icelandish as possible, and of Hottentot as Hottentot, is in this respect at the opposite pole from Dryden's. If readers of the 1700 *Fables* wanted fourteenth-century flavors, they could get them easily enough by turning to the back of the folio volume where they would find reprinted the Middle English texts from which Dryden had worked.

Thus, in respect to allusions, references, and idioms which would have once been clear to readers of an original poem but would not be so now to buyers of his new translations, Dryden came to prefer an out-and-out modern adaptation; in translating Juvenal and Persius, indeed, he used footnotes; but he never relished the device and preferred if possible to let a poem speak for itself in a completely self-explanatory manner.

> O newe Scariot, newe Genylon,
> False dissymulour, o Greek Synon,
> That broughtest Troy al outrely to sorwe!
> (4417–9)

cries out the Nun's Priest, apostrophizing the wicked fox in his tale. "O vile subverter of the Gallic reign, More false than Gano was to Charlemagne"—so runs part of Dryden's translation, which avoids a footnote on Genylon by imitating the very manner in which Chaucer had identified the possibly recondite Sinon.

A passage in "The Knight's Tale" shows Dryden faced with a proverbial expression of the Middle Ages:

> We witen nat what thing we preyen heere:
> We faren as he that dronke is as a mous.
> A dronke man woot wel he hath an hous,
> But he noot which the righte wey is thider,
> And to a dronke man the wey is slider.
> And certes, in this world so faren we;
> We seken faste after felicitee,
> But we goon wrong ful often, trewely.
> (1260–7)

The mouse presents any translator with a problem that, it seems to me, can be clearly stated. To retain this bibulous animal will gain pictur-

9. J. U. Nicolson, *The Canterbury Tales, Rendered into Modern English* (Covici, Friede, 1934), p. 342.

esqueness but at the expense of possibly distracting a reader's attention from the main point of the passage, the irony of human prayer, and of human forethought generally. Most Chaucer-modernizers plump for the picturesque, and translate the line in question by some variant of "We fare as he that drunk is as a mouse"; but one, F. W. Pitt-Taylor, adds a footnote: "Or, as we should say, 'drunk as a lord' "; [1] while another, F. Whitmore, contrives the couplet:

> Like mice are we for whom the trap is set,
> Like drunken men who their own way forget— [2]

a desperate expedient. Dryden's dropping of the archaic metaphor:

> we know not for what things to pray.
> Like drunken sots about the streets we roam—
> Well knows the sot he has a certain home, etc.

is thoroughly characteristic of his methods.

But though he eschewed the sort of language which might call for marginal exegesis, it would be a mistake to suppose that the phraseology of Dryden's translations is always equally unrelated to that of his originals. One of the characteristic features of the style which Dryden, working with materials derived from Milton and the Elizabethans, created and caused to dominate English poetry for a century after his death is its occasional Latinity; and it is accordingly not surprising to find later commentators on Dryden's translations from Roman authors complaining that he is sometimes "overliteral" in his rendition of these poets. Take the following epic simile from the second book of Dryden's *Aeneid:*

> Thus, when a flood of fire by wind is borne,
> Crackling it rolls, and mows the standing corn;
> Or deluges, descending on the plains,
> Sweep o'er the yellow year, destroy the pains
> Of lab'ring oxen and the peasant's gains.
> (406–10)

"The pains of lab'ring oxen" is based on Virgil's *bovum labores,* and has been recently condemned as "a perversion of the Latin by . . . over-vivid translation" [3]—conveying, as it does, by a kind of pun on the translator's part, two possible meanings of the Latin noun *labores.*

Here, unless I am mistaken, some of that delicate regretfulness, that *desiderium,* which critics have stated that Dryden missed in bringing over Virgil, seems to have unaccountably found its way into this pic-

---

1. *The Canterbury Tales Rendered into Modern English* (1884), p. 46.
2. *The Canterbury Tales. A Selective Version* (Dorance, 1939), p. 36.
3. Reuben A. Brower, "Dryden's Poetic Diction and Virgil," *Philological Quarterly, 18* (1939), 214. The article is a useful collection of instances, but needlessly hostile (I think) to Dryden, whom Brower has treated more cordially elsewhere (see, for example, his "An Allusion to Europe; Dryden and Tradition," *ELH, 19* [1952], 38–48).

ture of the vicissitudes, the fires and floods, to which husbandmen are occasionally subject. "Pains," emphatic because it bears the rhyme and because the phrase of which it is part breaks over into the next line, sharpens the sense of sorrow for the loss of something that had been so hard, so costly in trouble and effort, to achieve. The results of the beasts' toil, the act of toiling itself, the physical distress involved—all these shades of meaning implicit in "pains" are carried over and linked by alliteration to the peasant of the next line. The expression "pains of oxen" may be typically neoclassic in form, and capable of providing a special pleasure of recognition to the Latinical reader; but it seems to function quite as well in the English passage as that other example of "stock poetic diction" which adjoins it, the phrase "the yellow year." Indeed, while the passage is before us, it is worth noting how Dryden moves from the specific, direct, matter-of-fact "standing corn" to this lovely periphrasis which, though it refers to the same thing, suggests by its wide inclusiveness that a whole season has been blotted out of the calendar by the flood. From the farmer's point of view, that is just what has happened.

If "pains of lab'ring oxen," however, has laid Dryden open to a charge of "over-vividness," the more usual objection to certain Latinate conventions of his style has been that they are not vivid *enough*. "In practically all the . . . periphrases for which there is a Virgilian original," writes the critic just quoted, "Dryden's equivalent is at once more vague and more abstract. For example, when Virgil speaks of *salsus fluctus,* we have a concrete impression of the sea—'salty waves.' In Dryden's 'briny draught' we get no sense impression whatever. 'Draught,' in particular, is one of the most colorless words that could be found in English for 'water' or 'a drink of water.' " [4] So colorless, in fact (one might comment), that it was chosen by that colorless poet Keats for a notoriously colorless passage in his "Ode to a Nightingale"—"Oh for a draught of vintage . . ." But a glance at the passage in which Dryden uses the allegedly vague and abstract "briny draught" is more relevant to the matter in hand. An angry captain has thrown overboard his incompetent pilot during a boat race:

> Hardly his head the plunging pilot rears,
> Clogg'd with his clothes, and cumber'd with his
>   years:
> Now dropping wet, he climbs the cliff with pain.
> The crowd, that saw him fall and float again,
> Shout from the distant shore; and loudly laugh'd
> To see his heaving breast disgorge the briny draught.
>   (v, 231–6)

4. Brower, "Dryden's Poetic Diction," pp. 214–15. Cf. *Aeneid,* v, 182, 237–8.

Remember that from those last two words we are supposed to "get no sense impression whatever"!

It is not surprising to find the diction of Dryden's translations controversial, however; for this diction is connected with attitudes of mind, ways of looking at the world, groups of related emotions which are, as we should expect, rooted in Dryden's own age, and which accordingly gave offense when the attitudes of that age yielded to the Romantic and Victorian sensibility. Anything to do with observation of nature—taking "nature" in the sense of "landscape" or "scenery"—is naturally a very sensitive area in these disputes; for readers of the classics in any age will of course see the objects described in them partly through the lenses of their own sensibility. In general, nature was important to Dryden's age as it related to human life and purpose (cf. the catalogue of trees discussed earlier in this chapter); while for the romantics it came to have an essentially religious validity through its mysteriousness. Perhaps none of the authors whom Dryden translated had received themselves the specifically romantic shudder from trees and pools, mountains and forest glades; but if the nineteenth century thought they had, that fact was enough to throw Dryden's language, and his powers as a translator, into question.

Here, for example, are two versions of the same passage in the *Aeneid,* the first by Rolfe Humphries, whose manner derives from Tennyson, the second by Dryden:

> In a bay's deep curve
> They find a haven, where the water lies,
> With never a ripple. A little island keeps
> The sea-swell off, and the waves break on its sides
> And slide back harmless. The great cliffs come down
> Steep to deep water, and the background shimmers,
> Darkens and shines, the tremulous aspen moving
> And the dark fir pointing still. And there is a cave
> Under the overhanging rocks, alive
> With water running fresh, a home of the Nymphs,
> With benches for them, cut from the living stone.
> No anchor is needed here for weary ships,
> No mooring cable.
>
> (p. 9)

> Within a long recess there lies a bay:
> An island shades it from the rolling sea,
> And forms a port secure for ships to ride;
> Broke by the jutting land, on either side,
> In double streams the briny waters glide.
> Betwixt two rows of rocks a sylvan scene

Appears above, and groves forever green;
A grot is form'd beneath, with mossy seats,
To rest the Nereids, and exclude the heats.
Down thro' the crannies of the living walls
The crystal streams descend in murm'ring falls:
No haulsers need to bind the vessels here,
Nor bearded anchors; for no storms they fear.

(1, 228–40)

It is clear that what interests Dryden in the passage is the sense of order and well-being ("a port secure," "groves forever green," "exclude the heats," "the crystal streams," "No haulsers . . . Nor bearded anchors"). What interests Humphries, on the other hand, is the strangeness of the setting: "The background shimmers . . . the dark fir pointing still"—at what? one asks. The choice of language, the liberties taken with literal sense, inevitably reflect these divergent interests.

Commenting on Dryden's version, Mark Van Doren, the poet's most distinguished recent critic, reflects the nineteenth-century position: "In these 'briny waters,' 'sylvan scenes,' and 'crystal streams' are the beginnings of the stereotyped Nature which graced the verse of England for at least two generations . . . Dryden supplied himself with a kind of natural furniture with which he could stock any house of verse that seemed to him bare. He laid in a fund of phrases with which he could expand any passage that seemed to him curt." [5]

It is possible to argue with the details of this analysis. If "beginnings" implies, for example, that Dryden invented the three phrases quoted, then it is relevant to point out that "sylvan scene" occurs (in the plural) in Lauderdale's earlier translation of the same passage (1, 171); that it had formerly been used by Milton in *Paradise Lost* (IV, 140); and that Milton—who probably exercised just as much influence over the next two generations of poets as Dryden did, if not more—took it, by a kind of pun similar to some of Ezra Pound's in *Personae,* from the very Latin passage Dryden is here translating (*"tum silvis scaena coruscis"*). ("Crystal stream," moreover, occurs in *The Faerie Queene* [1, Canto i, 34], and resembles similar phrases in Spenser, such as "crystal flood," "crystal waves," "crystal brook," and "crystal wells.") If "for at least two generations" implies a contrast between Dryden and poets of much more recent vintage, then it is relevant to mention the presence of the stereotyped "crystal flood" in Keats and Wordsworth,[6] and of the stereotyped "sylvan scene" in "The Waste Land" (l. 98).

Debating points aside, however, I think that the main drift of Van

---

5. *Poetry of Dryden* (1946), pp. 55–6. For the quotation from Humphries, see his *Aeneid of Virgil* (Scribner's, 1951).

6. See Wordsworth, "Armenian Lady's Love," l. 96; "White Doe," l. 150; and "Excursion," IV, l. 1044; Keats, "Stanzas to Miss Wylie," l. 3.

Doren's discussion is right enough, despite the fact that he seems unduly hard on a gracefully executed passage; but his comments on the style need extension, I feel, in two directions.

In the first place, poetry being itself a convention, it is perhaps both natural and desirable that conventions within its language should exist; and should rise, flourish, and decay from time to time. The passage in Chesterfield's letters cited by Douglas Bush in mockery of eighteenth-century verse:

> poetry is a more noble and sublime way of expressing one's thoughts. For example, in prose you would say very properly, "it is twelve of the clock at noon," to mark the middle of the day; but this would be too plain and flat in poetry; and you would rather say, "the Chariot of the Sun has already finished half its course." In prose you would say, "The beginning of the morning or the break of day"; but that would not do in verse; and you must rather say, "Aurora spread her rosy mantle." Aurora, you know, is the goddess of the morning. This is what is called poetical diction.[7]

can be paralleled a century later (though less amusingly) in Matthew Arnold's description of

> what may be called the poetical vocabulary, as distinguished from the vocabulary of common speech and of modern prose: I mean, such expressions as *perchance* for *perhaps, spake* for *spoke, aye* for *ever, don* for *put on, charmèd* for *charm'd,* and thousands of others.[8]

Such conventions, it seems to me, can reflect the legitimate interests, the stance taken toward a subject-matter, of a period, a genre, or a poet; and simply to show that they are used in a specific passage is inconclusive evidence as to poetic merit.

In the second place, the conventions about nature used in Dryden's *Aeneid* are related to those of Western epic in general, to the "whale road" of *Beowulf* or the recurrent "the sun sank and the ways were darkened" of the *Odyssey*. While it is true that Dryden is somewhat less detailed than Virgil in this passage, and Virgil less so than is the passage of Homer he was imitating, the degree of concreteness in sketching the scenic background in the three poems may indicate differences in theme and subject matter, rather than a degeneration of style.

Finally, there is the all-important question of the skill with which a set of conventions has been manipulated, and here I think Dryden's treatment of the port would stand up well under detailed analysis. The principle on which he organizes the landscape is duality: the ocean

---

7. *Mythology and the Romantic Tradition,* p. 20; see *Letters of Philip Dormer Stanhope* (ed. Dobrée, 1932), No. 641 (1739); *2, 362.*
8. "Last Words" (1862), in *Essays* (London, 1914), p. 390.

and the spring, the cave beneath and the groves above. This principle is expressed in patterns of the verses themselves. For example, as the rolling ocean approaches the bay,

> In double streams the briny waters glide;

while within the cave, on the other hand,

> The crystal streams descend in murm'ring falls.

The briny-crystal contrast brings out the utility of the anchorage to the Trojan mariners; the close parallelism draws the hostile ocean itself into the mood of the static, inviting pastoral landscape. The storm raised by Juno has just subsided and the expeditionary force is about to be subjected to Carthaginian temptations; as a transitional passage, Dryden's seems admirable.

Besides his adjustment of archaic allusion, his Latinism, and his stock diction for landscape, Dryden's occasional employment of personification is a fourth "period" feature of his translating methods that has been sometimes attacked. Critics, notably Saintsbury and Housman, have censured him for replacing Chaucer's now famous line about the smiler with the knife under the cloak with *three* lines on a capitalized abstraction, Hypocrisy; and certainly Dryden's departure from the methods that would suggest themselves to a literalist is·very striking in this instance. As with the "briny draught" passage in Virgil, I do not think the departure can be adequately discussed without some reference to the immediate context of Chaucer's line. The passage comes in a description of the Temple of Mars in "The Knight's Tale":

> Ther saugh I first the derke ymaginyng
> Of Felonye, and al the compassyng;
> The crueel Ire, reed as any gleede;
> The pykepurs, and eek the pale Drede;
> The smylere with the knyf under the cloke; . . .
> (1995–8)

Dryden, dropping the pick-purse, and bringing Ire and Dread into one line, renders the passage as follows:

> There saw I how the secret felon wrought,
> And treason lab'ring in the traitor's thought,
> And midwife Time the ripen'd plot to murder brought.
> There the red Anger dared the pallid Fear;
> Next stood Hypocrisy with holy leer;
> Soft smiling, and demurely looking down,
> But hid the dagger underneath the gown: . . .
> (II, 560–6)

The structure of Dryden's version is based on the introduction of paradox into the images of the passage, which now include two innovations: a birth and a priest. The first new image has three parts: conception ("how the secret felon wrought"), gestation ("lab'ring"), and parturition ("midwife," "ripen'd," etc.). The paradox is that what is being born, being created, is murder; similarly the second new image, that of the priest, contrasts what we would ordinarily expect with a brutal inversion of natural functions: the dagger underneath the clerical gown. The pivotal line of the passage, "There the red Anger dared the pallid Fear," looks backward in "Anger" at the plotting assassin; and forward in "Fear" at the soft smiles of the even more covert killer.

Dryden's passage, in other words, is balanced; Chaucer's is cumulative. Beginning with Felony, a milder conception than treason or murder, Chaucer proceeds through two personified emotions and the pick-purse to his smiler with the knife. Actually, though his final image has a concentration and intensity somewhat dissipated in the translation, his preceding ones lack the visual and metaphorical energy of Dryden.

Such energy in the use of personification (by no means a necessarily "frigid" device) has been sometimes recognized by critics. Of another passage in Dryden's version of the same poem, a description of the Temple of Venus—

> Before the palace gate, in careless dress,
> And loose array, sat portress Idleness;
> There, by the fount, Narcissus pin'd alone;
> There Samson was, with wiser Solomon,
> And all the mighty names by love undone—
> (II, 500–4)

W. H. Williams writes:

> Here we may notice the picturesque addition of the phrase "in careless Dress and loose Array," to the bare "porter Ydelnesse," and the change to the feminine in "Portress Idleness"; the legend of Narcissus sufficiently suggested by the touches "by the Fount" and "pin'd alone"; the substitution of Samson for Hercules, partly to pair with Solomon, partly as a better example of the power of love; . . .[9]

It might be added that "Samson" pairs with "Solomon" in sound as well as sense, and that both words beautifully anticipate the melody coming in the next line "by love undone." Indeed the phrase "mighty names," by force of the whole passage, takes on a double implication: it becomes not only a periphrasis for "mighty heroes," but also, more literally, a

---

9. "Dryden's Palamon and Arcite and the Knight's Tale," *Modern Language Review, 9* (1914), 323.

suggestion that the names in themselves have had (like spells or runes) a potency which they are now losing under the influence of love. Another set of sound echoes links similarly "portress," "Idleness," and "Narcissus," and suggests that the gateway to the palace of love involves both indolence and introspection. In passages like this, Dryden's experience of the author he is translating has been enriched by his own talents as an English Augustan poet of the first magnitude; Chaucer, read through the spectacles of Dryden's age, has become for him an opportunity and a challenge.

Some of Dryden's changes in literal sense, then, reflect the pressure of long poetic or philosophic traditions; others respond to the contemporary situation in English poetry in the late seventeenth century. In those two classes of changes, the poet confronts the past and the present: the long echoing corridors of lettered Europe, and the urgent immediate expectations of coffeehouse circles in modern England. Both pressures are, however, in a sense external to his real problem as a translator: the original itself; and there are occasions when the original would have been, in Dryden's eyes, as ill served by fidelity to its mere *words* as would the European tradition or the contemporary English reader.

As examples of such occasions I shall give two from passages in the *Aeneid* where Dryden is leaning on the most recent version to have been made in English before his, that of the Earl of Lauderdale; for Lauderdale is somewhat more literal than Dryden and yet, in the passages I am going to quote, very similar to him in general method. What he makes of the Latin can therefore serve as a convenient foil to Dryden. Dryden's use of Lauderdale, incidentally, has been the subject of unfriendly comment. Mark Van Doren writes: "By his own confession, he kept the manuscript of the Earl of Lauderdale's translation by him and 'consulted it as often as I doubted of my author's sense,' or as often, more likely, as he felt pressed for time. Some two hundred lines of that nobleman's version he appropriated without any alteration at all, and some eight hundred came over only slightly recast." [1]

The lines that came over slightly recast are more interesting to an investigator of Dryden's methods than those he appropriated unaltered, and the examples I shall give fall into the former category. (It seems unnecessary to suppose, however, that Dryden's use of Lauderdale in connection with about 7 per cent of the total number of lines in his *Aeneid* was, any more than his similar though less frequent use of Sandys, Waller, Denham, Ogilby, and others, due primarily to indolence.[2])

A dramatic moment in the third book of the *Aeneid* is the voyagers' first sight of Italy. It came at daybreak:

1. *Poetry of Dryden*, p. 101; cf. Dryden's *Essays*, ed. Ker, *2*, 235.
2. See above, Ch. i, p. 3.

iamque rubescebat stellis Aurora fugatis,
cum procul obscuros collis humilemque videmus
Italiam.

(III, 521–3)

As important as the words themselves in conveying the drama of the experience is their arrangement, especially the delaying of the crucial "Italiam" to the end of a clause, and to the beginning of a new line. Here the flexibility of Latin word order allowed the climax.

Focusing on the meaning, rather than the order, of the words in the crucial clause, Lauderdale translated as follows:

The blushing Morn had put the Stars to flight,
When little Hills from far salute our Sight.
Then we the Plains of *Italy* descry'd, . . .

(III, 578–80)

Dryden's version apparently owes a verb and a phrase to Lauderdale's, but it is less literal, rendering the epithet *obscuros* by a newly created simile, "like bluish mists"; and above all, it reflects Virgil's sense of climax:

And now the rising morn with rosy light
Adorns the skies, and puts the stars to flight;
When we from far, like bluish mists, descry
The hills, and then the plains, of Italy.

(III, 682–5)

Virgil's delayed emphasis in "Italiam" is matched not only by the use of "Italy" for a final rhyme (and a slant rhyme at that), but also by the delaying breaks in the rhythm (secured partly by enjambment and partly by two interrupting phrases) which precede this last word of the second couplet.

A short speech of the Sibyl's in Book VI will serve to illustrate another sort of Virgilian felicity, also not easily rendered by literal methods. Here again, as the opening phrase and all the rhyme words show, Dryden had consulted his Lauderdale:

dicite, felices animae, tuque, optime vates
quae regio Anchisen, quis habet locus? illius ergo
venimus et magnos Erebi tranavimus amnes.

(VI, 669–71)

The repetition of m, n, and a sounds in that third line is a striking feature of the poetry. It imparts, I think, a fixed marmoreal quality to the Sibyl's statement, and emphasizes, by the weight it gives to "magnos," the supernatural distance of the expedition. To all this Lauderdale seems fairly insensitive:

> Say happy Souls, and you bless'd Poet, say,
> What shady grove? What pleasant place? What way
> Leads to *Anchises?* For his only sake
> We hither came, and cross'd the *Stygian* Lake.
>
> (VI, 815–18)

Compared to Lauderdale, Dryden again is freer with dictionary equivalents: we can locate words corresponding to "vates," "regio," "locus," and "Erebi," more easily in Lauderdale than in Dryden, who renders the passage as follows:

> Say, happy souls, divine Musaeus, say,
> Where lives Anchises, and where lies our way
> To find the hero, for whose only sake
> We sought the dark abodes, and cross'd the bitter
> lake?
>
> (VI, 908–11)

In two respects the later translator has improved on his predecessor: the entire speech is embraced in one sentence, instead of being chopped up as in Lauderdale's second and third lines; and Dryden's final line, with its beautiful balance, alliteration, and assonance is an improvement not only in musical effect but in imaginative and evocative phrasing. The underworld with all its wry and shadowy associations is present in the words "dark abodes" and "bitter lake"; while the melody of "venimus et magnos Erebi tranavimus amnes" has evoked an answering melody. I may add that I find Dryden's success at this point no better illustrated by contrast with his forgotten precursor than by contrast with the much more recent, indeed the current, versions of Cecil Day-Lewis ("We have come here, Crossing the great rivers of the Underworld, to see him") and Rolfe Humphries ("For him we have traversed Erebus' great rivers"). Dryden's aim was to translate poetry, not simply the words of poems.

2. *Lines*

The line is so obvious and so basic an organizing agent in poetry generally that upon some translators it has exerted an irrational, almost hypnotic influence, causing the production of those line-for-line versions which still occasionally appear. The two examples just given from Dryden's Virgil would suggest that, while Dryden does not of course bind himself to the structure of his originals in any artificial, a priori manner, he is conscious of the effects in them of line division, among these being the occasional quasi-autonomy of an individual line; and that this consciousness can affect his own procedures.

For one thing, there occur instances where he adopts a line of his original. This process, possible, of course, only in the Chaucer versions, is sometimes exact:

> Black was his beard, and manly was his face

> Up rose the sun, and up rose Emily

> The slayer of himself yet saw I there

sometimes approximate:

> Now up, now doun, as boket in a welle
> Now up, now down, as buckets in a well

> For pitee renneth soone in gentil herte
> And pity soonest runs in gentle minds

> "Why woldestow be deed," thise wommen crye,
> "And haddest gold ynough, and Emelye?"
> "Why wouldst thou go," with one consent they cry,
> "When thou hadst gold enough, and Emily?"

I have noticed about a dozen such parallels in the twenty-four hundred lines of "Palamon and Arcite." [3] Admirers of Chaucer who are also enemies of the Augustans naturally find among such lines Dryden's greatest triumphs as a translator—see Housman's comments, for example, in his *Name and Nature of Poetry*. As with several of the examples I have given, the lines chosen have an epigrammatic or aphoristic flavor. In such adoptions, Dryden is at his closest, in method, to the general run of nineteenth- and twentieth-century Chaucer-modernizers; and it is significant that such methods occur so infrequently in his work. Actually, he uses the text of Chaucer in this respect in more or less the same way he used some earlier translation of Virgil for his own *Aeneid*. If he found that Chaucer had already—in an occasional line or two— written his own best translation into modern English, he no more hesitated to take advantage of this fact than he did to accept a line for his Virgil from Lauderdale or Ogilby.

More typical of his methods as translator are those cases where a line, or perhaps the principal part of a line, in his original has had an obvious grammatical or rhetorical influence on Dryden's line structure. The following occurs in the description of the Elysian Fields in the *Aeneid*:

> solemque suum, sua sidera norunt
>
> (VI, 641)

3. "Palamon and Arcite," I, 274–5 ("The Knight's Tale," 1115–16) ; II, 37–8 (1491–2) ; II, 71–2 (1521–2) ; II, 82 (1533) ; II, 157 (1614) ; II, 332 (1761) ; II, 448–9 (1893–4) ; II, 544–5 (1981–2) ; II, 576 (2005) ; III, 40 (2130) ; III, 145 (2223) ; III, 190 (2273) ; III, 418 (2469) ; III, 873–4 (2835–6) ; and cf. also I, 591–4 (1429–32) ; III, 388 (2449), a misunderstanding of the original.

Dryden translates:

> Stars of their own, and their own suns, they know.
> (VI, 872)

Even here, where the imitation is close in some respects, the heavenly bodies have changed places, and Virgil's sun has become plural in the translation. The latter change gives the new line a more perfect balance, in a way that for Virgil (because the plural of *sol* would not correspond in form to *sidera*) would have been impossible, even if desired. At the same time, the very idea of more than one sun is arresting—though I suppose Dryden's line means not several suns at once, but a new one each day—and to reverse the position of "stars" and "suns" in the translation would be anticlimactic. Finally, Dryden cannot have *one* sun and imitate Virgil's rhetoric so easily here, because of the need in English for an indefinite article.

Farther from the manner of the original, though an obvious line-for-line correspondence in general content, is this from "The Knight's Tale" (a detail in Theseus' insignia):

> The Mynotaur, which that he slough in Crete.
> (980)

> His Cretan fight, the conquer'd Minotaur,
> (I, 116)

The new arrangement is more clearly emphatic, impersonal, and heroic in tone: more is at work here than the mere fact that such a collocation as "which that he slough" defies importation without change.

Even where line-for-line correspondence is abandoned, as it usually is, the structure of a foreign line may still affect the translation. The compression of Latin verse, and the magnificence of Lucretian rhetoric, are, for example, well illustrated in the following pair of lines from the third book of the *De Rerum Natura,* a problem for any translator:

> Scipiadas, belli fulmen, Carthaginis horror
> Ossa dedit terrae proinde ac famul infimus
>   esset.
> (III, 1034–5)

Dryden's version manages to keep the phrase translating "belli fulmen" at the center of a line and that translating "Carthaginis horror" at the conclusion of one:

> The Roman chief, the Carthaginian dread,
> Scipio, the thunderbolt of war, is dead,
> And, like a common slave, by fate in triumph led.
> (III, 248–50)

His treatment, moreover, preserves, despite expansion, a kind of tight-
ness and a sense of climax which less attention to the line-structure of
the Latin is always in danger of losing. Compare, for example,
Trevelyan:

> The Scipios' offspring, thunderbolt of war,
> Terror of Carthage, gave his bones to the earth
> As though he were the meanest household slave.
>
> (p. 125)

Another way line-structure of an original can influence Dryden occurs when a group of related, parallel lines—such as a series of invoca-
tions—are to be translated. A line already cited, Dryden's translation of
"nocturnisque Hecate triviis ululata per urbes" by "Thou Hecate
hearken from thy dark abodes," is a part of such a collocation; the translation follows Virgil in giving a line to Dido's appeals to the sun, Juno,
and Hecate:

> Thou Sun, who view'st at once the world below;
> Thou Juno, guardian of the nuptial vow;
> Thou Hecate hearken from thy dark abodes!
> Ye Furies, fiends, and violated gods, . . .
>
> (IV, 872-5)

The "Hecate" line, a bold departure from the Latin both in its organization and its sense, achieves a rapidity appropriate to the feverish speech
of the love-tormented queen, a rapidity doubtless impossible had the
full sense of "nocturnisque," etc., been given. Here Dryden imitates
less what Virgil actually said than the fact that he said it *in lines*.

A vivid awareness of the individual line, in fact, was probably one of
the advantages Dryden derived from his age (by contrast to more recent times) for the translation of the particular authors he had selected.
With some of the lines he adopted word-for-word or almost word-for-
word from Chaucer a line of his own like "Fresh as the month, and as
the morning fair" ("Palamon and Arcite," I, 182, from a description
of Emily) is not in the least out of harmony. To a classic design, like
Homer's Κάστορά θ'ἱππόδαμον καὶ πὺξ ἀγαθὸν Πολυδεύκεα, it marries an
Anglo-Saxon directness of diction. A cento of such lines, in which, as
in "We sought the dark abodes and cross'd the bitter lake," noun-
adjective combinations of varying metrical structure balance against
each other, could be compiled from Dryden's *Aeneid* alone:

> Swift Helymus, and lovely Panopes
>
> (V, 394)

> To the sweet banks of yon forbidden shore
>
> (VI, 505)

In secret solitude and myrtle shades
(VI, 599)

When his refulgent arms flash'd thro' the shady plain
(VI, 660)

Of polish'd iv'ry this, that of transparent horn
(VI, 1236)

With yawning mouths, and with half-open'd eyes
(VIII, 544)

His broken axletrees and blunted war
(VIII, 572)

All-seeing sun, and thou, Ausonian soil
(XII, 266)

3. Couplets

But of course the most characteristic feature of English Augustan poetry is not so much the single line as the closed couplet. In Chaucer's couplets, rhyme, for example, is often less organic to his rhetoric [4] than in Pope's or Dryden's; so that we find Dryden tending to rearrange materials which in Chaucer had merely cut across the loose-linking rhymes:

Lo Catoun, which that was so wys a man,
Seyde he nat thus, "Ne do no fors of dremes?"
("Nun's Priest's Tale," 4130–1)

Cato was in his time accounted wise
And he condemns them all for empty lies.
(162–3)

Myn is the drenchyng in the see so wan;
Myn is the prison in the derke cote . . .
("Knight's Tale," 2456–7)

Mine is the shipwreck in a wat'ry sign;
And in an earthy, the dark dungeon mine.
(III, 401–2)

Similarly, Dryden occasionally gathers into a pair of closed couplets what had been more loosely disposed by his author:

Myn is the ruyne of the hye halles,
The fallynge of the toures and of the walles

4. Cf. W. K. Wimsatt, Jr., "One Relation of Rhyme to Reason: Alexander Pope," *Modern Language Quarterly*, 5 (1944), 323–38.

Upon the mynour or the carpenter.
I slow Sampsoun, shakynge the piler; . . .
("Knight's Tale," 2463–6)

By me king's palaces are push'd to ground,
And miners crush'd beneath their mines are found.
'Twas I slew Samson, when the pillar'd hall
Fell down and crush'd the many with the fall.
(III, 414–17)

A further difference from Chaucer's couplets, however, is the presence in Dryden of alexandrine and triplet. One of his triplets sometimes corresponds to a four-line passage in the original:

O Cupide, out of alle charitee!
O regne, that wolt no felawe have with thee!
Ful sooth is seyd that love ne lordshipe
Wol noght, his thankes, have no felaweshipe.
("Knight's Tale," 1623–6)

O Love! thou sternly dost thy pow'r maintain,
And wilt not bear a rival in thy reign:
Tyrants and thou all fellowship disdain.
(II, 166–8)

or sometimes to a two-line passage:

And seyde hym thus: "If thou tomorwe wende,
Thow shalt be dreynt; my tale is at an ende."
("Nun's Priest's Tale," 4271–2)

"I come, thy genius, to command thy stay;
Trust not the winds, for fatal is the day,
And death unhop'd attends the wat'ry way."
(312–14)

In the first of the two examples, the triplet diminishes the garrulity of the original, its third line replacing a couplet. In the second, where Chaucer's superiority seems to me evident, something like an opposite process is at work; for "fatal" and "death" repeat each other; while the idea of drowning is scarcely reinforced, in this context (a monitory dream), by being spread out over "the winds" and "the wat'ry way." Much the same point could be made about the appearance of flexibility afforded by alexandrines, whose advantages and disadvantages to the translator similarly tend to cancel each other out.[5]

5. In his *Aeneid,* as Joseph Bottkol has shown in an unpublished Harvard dissertation, "Dryden's Translations from Classical Verse" (1937), Dryden tends to combine groups of couplets or triplets, in varying patterns, as units of statement. In his Lucretius, even fourteeners can be found.

Triplets and alexandrines, in fact, can be regarded as symptoms of a degree of looseness occasionally present in Dryden's translations—a looseness which the very nature of the neoclassical couplet did not encourage. The tendency of this kind of couplet, partly because it presented clearly marked termini, was to become more tightly packed:

> Mine is the shipwreck in a wat'ry sign;
> And in an earthy, the dark dungeon mine.

To Chaucer's statement the mention of astrological "signs" has been added, while the slight tautology present in "drenchyng" and "see," and in "prison" and "cote" has been squeezed out. After Dryden's time, this tightening and packing tendency increased in the couplets of Pope and Johnson, a development which can be shown where either of the latter poets operates as translator on material that had already been worked by Dryden: specifically, the first book of Homer's *Iliad,* and the Third and Tenth Satires of Juvenal.

Pope's couplets in his *Iliad* are a contrast with Dryden's in his fragment of the same poem, being more compressed, more abstract, more balanced and antithetical, and sometimes wittier. Here, for instance, are a pair of couplets:

> *Dryden:* Whate'er by force of arms the soldier got,
> Is each his own, by dividend of lot.
>   (I, 188–9)

> *Pope:* The spoils of cities razed, and warriors
> slain,
> We share with justice, as with toil we gain.
>   (I, 159–60)

And here a pair of lines:

> *Dryden:* We need not such a friend, nor fear we such
> a foe.
>   (I, 260)

> *Pope:* Thy aid we need not; and thy threats defy.
>   (I, 226)

In the first example, Pope has the air of saying *more* than Dryden, and with greater symmetry; in the second, where Dryden has an alexandrine, Pope is more succinct. In the following passages, Dryden's expression is more vivid, Pope's more tightly knit:

> *Dryden:*   for still, above the rest,
> Thy hook'd rapacious hands usurp the best;

Tho' mine are first in fight, to force the
prey,
And last sustain the labors of the day.
(1, 246–9)

Pope: Thine in each conquest is the wealthy prey,
Tho' mine the sweat and danger of the day.
(1, 217–8)

Pope's manner involves the danger of vagueness if significant universality is not achieved:

Pope: Not half so dear were Clytemnestra's charms,
When first her blooming beauties bless'd my
arms.
(1, 143–4)

Dryden: Not Clytemnestra's self in beauty's bloom
More charm'd, or better plied the various
loom.
(1, 169–70)

One feels that Pope has not improved matters by obliterating the concreteness of the loom. Yet the obliteration is in harmony with his general approach to Homer, which is more abstract than Dryden's throughout *Iliad*, 1. Differing theories as to the nature of Homeric poetry had something to do with this contrast; but so, I think, did Pope's ambition to excel earlier English poets in "correctness." Correctness involved a stricter attention to the archetypal form, one might call it, of the neoclassic couplet.

That archetypal form is nowhere better exhibited than in the finest work of Samuel Johnson; and the points at which his imitations of Juvenal's satires approach closest in content to Dryden's translations of them consequently furnish an epitome of the evolution, over two generations, of that particular verse form in English poetry. By this I do not mean that Johnson's results are always necessarily better than those of Dryden, who has his own contrasting excellences; but simply that Johnson, in the examples I shall give, is more fully aware of what can be done with the couplet as a means of statement—of how a single distich can be most efficiently loaded with implications.

Wherever Johnson and Dryden use the same Juvenalian raw material, Johnson is generally either briefer than his predecessor, or meatier. In the following pair of couplets he is meatier:

Dryden: Now while my friend, just ready to depart,
Was packing all his goods in one poor cart; . . .
(III, 17–18)

Johnson: While Thales waits the wherry that contains
Of dissipated wealth the small remains, . . .
(*London,* 19–20)

In the following he is more compact:

Dryden: What scene so desart, or so full of fright,
As tow'ring houses tumbling in the night, . . .
But worse than all, the clatt'ring tiles;
and worse
Than thousand padders, is the poets' curse;
Rogues that in dog days cannot rhyme forbear;
But without mercy read, and make you hear.
(III, 10–11, 13–16)

Johnson: Here falling houses thunder on your head,
And here a female atheist talks you dead.
(*London,* 17–18)

In the first Johnsonian couplet, "dissipated" expresses both a generalization and a judgment; in the second, the alliteration between "falling" and "female" and between "thunder" and "atheist," gives the effect of analysis, by purely symbolic means.

Even where Johnson uses more lines than Dryden a similar comparison can be made. When Dryden, for example, describes the terrors of a rich man who has to cross a heath at night with silver in his possession, and says that he

Shakes at the moonshine shadow of a rush,
And sees a redcoat rise from ev'ry bush: . . .
(X, 31–2)

the verse is easy, colloquial, and vivid; but the Great Moralist extracts more powerful, though less concrete, effects from the same situation—thus:

Now fears in dire vicissitude invade,
The rustling brake alarms, and quiv'ring shade,
Nor light nor darkness brings his pain relief,
One shows the plunder, and one hides the thief.
(*Vanity of Human Wishes,* 41–4)

The resources of the medium are here more amply exploited: the contrast between the abstract "fears in dire vicissitude" and the concrete "rustling brake" and "quiv'ring shade" (with "quiv'ring" also suggesting the physical state of the traveler); the varying types of parallelism in the second, third, and fourth lines; the exact placing of every word for maximum effect—everything attests Johnson's mastery. I will close these comparisons with a final illustration, in which the compression of the Johnsonian couplet operates like a lightning flash suddenly illuminating a psychological landscape:

> *Dryden:*   All Greece is one comedian: laugh, and they
> Return it louder than an ass can bray:
> Grieve, and they grieve; if you weep silently,
> There seems a silent echo in their eye: . . .
> (III, 170–3)

> *Johnson:*   To shake with laughter ere the jest
> they hear,
> To pour at will the counterfeited tear, . . .
> (*London,* 140–1)

4. *Verse Paragraphs*

To recapitulate briefly: the translator of poetry is always confronting a kind of chaos. He knows, if he is a sensitive reader, what the original says; or, to put it more exactly, he is aware of many aspects and features of its statement; but he is also aware that no other language can by any refinement of technique be made to say the same thing. He must therefore create a new artifact out of the rubble of dictionary meanings extracted from the old poem. Dryden, in doing so, allowed the European cultural tradition to serve as a matrix for his own creation; consulted the desires and expectations of late seventeenth-century readers; treated the literal sense of his authors with such liberties "as no Dutch commentator will forgive me"; [6] and always kept one eye on the more "untranslatable" aspects of his originals, the other on the esthetic requirements of his own new-minted poetry.

That this new poetry was to have a clearly marked structure of its own, and that the kinds of unity and continuity embodied in it would extend over wide areas, linking clusters of couplets together, has already been implied by a number of the more extended examples of Dryden's work which appear in this chapter; for example, by his translation of the "smiler with the knife" passage from "The Knight's Tale." His principal means of integration are, it seems to me, two: orchestration and imagery—means which he of course shares with any other first-rate poet, but, alas, with far fewer verse translators.

Dryden's ear has often been praised. Its usefulness to him as a translator is apparent not only in obviously onomatopoetic situations—

> Rustling of harness, rattling of the shield,
> Clatt'ring of armour, furbish'd for the field.

6. *Essays,* ed. Ker, *I,* 252.

Crowds to the castle mounted up the street,
Batt'ring the pavement with their coursers' feet—
("Palamon and Arcite," III, 445–8)

but also where sound echoes can be assimilated to, and made to strengthen, a chain of ideas. As an original poet, Dryden loved dialectics in verse; his skill comes out in the translations in all philosophic or argumentative passages, and especially, as we should expect, in his Lucretius. Here are three versions of a short passage from the third book of the *De Rerum Natura,* the first from the widely reprinted rendering by William Ellery Leonard; the second by the more recent translator R. C. Trevelyan (who has called Dryden's translations "intolerable travesties, devoid of almost everything that gives the original poems their greatness and individual charm" [7]) ; and the third by Dryden:

For stuff must be
That thus the after-generations grow,—
Though these, their life completed, follow thee:
And thus like thee are generations all—
Already fallen, or some time to fall.
So one thing from another rises ever;
And in fee-simple life is given to none,
But unto all in usufruct.
(1916 ed., pp. 127–8)

Matter is needed, that therefrom may grow
Succeeding generations: which yet all,
When they have lived their life, shall follow thee.
Thus it is all have perished in past times
No less than thou, and shall hereafter perish.
So one thing out of another shall not cease
For ever to arise; and life is given
To none in fee, to all in usufruct.
(p. 123)

New matter must be found for things to come,
And these must waste like thee, and follow Nature's doom.
All things, like thee, have time to rise and rot;
And from each other's ruin are begot:
For life is not confin'd to him or thee;
'Tis given to all for use, to none for property.
(III, 169–74)

Of these three, the first is neither attractive nor (except perhaps as a gloss on the Latin) readily understandable; the second seems to me more perspicuous but equally flat; whereas Dryden's is at once musical,

7. See the preface to his translation (Cambridge Univ. Press, 1937), p. xiv.

energetic, and at least as straightforward as Trevelyan's. Dryden has assimilated the legal metaphor of the last line better than the other translators; and his "rise . . . rot . . . ruin . . . begot" pattern intensifies the emotional force of the poetry and underlines its dialectic.

Sensitive to images, like any good poet, Dryden often allowed those he found in another author to operate as a stimulus on his own imagination, with a resultant enrichment of the texture of his translations. In the following brief bit from Chaucer, for example, the lion metaphor has been extended first by Dryden's verb "rends" and second by the alliteration of that verb with "rules" two lines previously:

> And softe unto hymselfe he seyde, "Fy
> Upon a lord that wol have no mercy,
> But been a leon, bothe in word and dede,
> To hem that been in repentaunce and drede,
> As wel as to a proud despitous man . . .
> ("Knight's Tale," 1773–7)

> And softly sighing to himself he said:
> "Curse on th' unpard'ning prince, whom tears can draw
> To no remorse; who rules by lions' law;
> And deaf to pray'rs, by no submission bow'd,
> Rends all alike; the penitent and proud!"
> (ii, 343–7)

In the following metamorphosis (Lycaon's) from Ovid, I have italicized phrases mainly owing to the inspiration of the translator; these are not only notable for enriching the pictorial quality of the event, but also for the ambiguities (of the word "brutal," for example) by means of which Lycaon's former character is shown to be implicit in his new one:

> The tyrant, in a fright, for shelter gains
> The neighb'ring fields, and scours along the plains.
> Howling he fled, and fain he would have spoke,
> But *human* voice *his brutal tongue* forsook.
> About his lips the gath'red foam he churns,
> And, breathing slaughters, still with rage he burns,
> But on the bleating flock his fury turns.
> His mantle, *now his hide,* with rugged hairs
> *Cleaves to his back; a famish'd face* he bears;
> His arms descend, *his shoulders sink away*
> *To multiply his legs for chase of prey.*
> He grows a wolf, his hoariness remains,
> And the same rage in other members reigns.

His eyes still sparkle in a narr'wer space,
His jaws retain the grin, and violence of face.
(*Metamorphoses*, 1, 305–19)

As a final example, here is a passage of which I have already quoted
the last line in another connection: Duke Theseus in "Palamon and
Arcite" riding home to Athens after devastating Thebes:

The red statue of Mars, with spere and targe,
So shyneth in his white baner large,
That alle the feeldes glyteren up and doun;
And by his baner born is his penoun
Of gold ful riche, in which ther was ybete
The Mynotaur, which that he slough in Crete.
(975–80)

And waved his royal banner in the wind:
Where in an argent field the God of War
Was drawn triumphant on his iron car;
Red was his sword, and shield, and whole attire,
And all the godhead seem'd to glow with fire;
Ev'n the ground glitter'd where the standard flew,
And the green grass was dyed to sanguine hue.
High on his pointed lance his pennon bore
His Cretan fight, the conquer'd Minotaur . . .
(1, 108–16)

The rhythmic cadences of the fourth line—"Red was his *sword*, and
shield, and whole *attire*"—ushering in the daring image of the dyed
grass, an image reinforced and bound together by a pattern of recurring
sounds; the combination of "High" with the alliterative "pointed," to
sweep the pennon aloft; the building of a climax both by transposition of
proper names and use of the alliterative "conquer'd" in the final line—
such skill gives some justification to Dryden's great editor Walter Scott
for referring to the poet, on occasion, as "glorious John." It is also indicative of the kind of results which can be produced when a poet with
a style of his own, and a genuine imaginative insight into an earlier
writer in another language, undertakes the task of verse translation.

IV

Dryden as Translator: Larger Problems

THE MOST IMPORTANT of Dryden's translations represent aspects of a larger literary and cultural problem: the assimilation by a modern age, that of the enlightenment in England, of memories of a heroic past. For Dryden's immediate predecessors, Shakespeare and Milton, the problem is evidently less acute; Milton can introduce into *Paradise Lost* images of the spice trade with the Orient or even of the sewers of London without violation of tone; while Shakespeare's *Coriolanus*, to use only one example, incorporates in an antique heroic context living representatives of the contemporary urban proletariat and small bourgeoisie. Even in Shakespeare's day, however, the appearance of a play like *The Knight of the Burning Pestle* shows the availability to literature of a sense of radical disparity between past and present;[1] by Dryden's time such feelings of disparity were evidently great enough to constitute both a danger and an opportunity to poets.

In general, the age developed two ways of dealing with its uncomfortably grand inheritance, and pursued both with some measure of success. The first was so to adjust the focus of its vision of the past as to lessen the risk of an uncomfortable intrusion of the present. This method involved a degree of purification and, consequently, of attenuation; but it did occasionally produce notable achievements, such as Dryden's *All for Love* and Pope's *Iliad,* instances which clearly show the purification process at work. In *All for Love,* by comparison with its Shakespearean predecessor, motivation is of a more consistently exalted kind; and anyone who will take the trouble of setting side by side Shakespeare's "The barge she sat on" and Dryden's corresponding "Her galley down the silver Cydnos rowed" will perceive the undercurrent of sexual imagery and suggestion characteristic of *Antony and Cleopatra* in many passages and far less characteristic of *All for Love.* As for Pope's *Iliad,* the classical pantheon in this poem has become both more godlike and more abstract than that of Homer; Apollo in Pope, for example, being presented as "a true deity and not a mere personifica-

---

1. It is interesting in this connection that the play evidently failed on the stage when first produced (about 1607), but won a warmer reception when revived twenty-five years later.

tion of the sun." [2] There are corresponding changes on the human level.

Despite some successes, however, the first approach to the heroic proved—as, for example, in Addison's *Cato*—relatively unfruitful compared with the second: the admixture, or adulteration, of epic, heroic, or classical materials with consciously modern, gross, and contrasting idiom and image, for the purpose of producing a spark like that across the gap between two charged electrical poles.

The nature of the illumination given forth by the spark varied with the proportions used in the adulterating mixture. Samuel Butler's *Hudibras,* and Cotton's travesty of Virgil, like Byron's "Vision of Judgment" later on, exhibit so gross an infiltration of the modern and the commonplace as to burlesque and by implication to invalidate their ostensibly heroic subject matter. In mixtures less gross but still predominantly "modern"—for example, *Mac Flecknoe* or *The Dunciad*—the effect is in an opposite direction: the heroic ideal still exists, and has value, but the contemporary scene presents at best a sad falling away from it. Yet a third type of mixture is represented by *The Rape of the Lock,* a mock-heroic poem in which the heroic predominates more heavily still. When Belinda, during a ritual in which she propitiates "the cosmetic powers," sits at her dressing table and "trembling begins the sacred rites of pride," the scene is invested for a moment with almost Satanic splendor; and the poem as a whole presents eighteenth-century London not as a pitiable travesty of the Homeric, the Virgilian, and the Miltonic worlds, but rather as a diminished analogue of the epic universe.[3]

The ambivalent attitude of Dryden's age toward the heroic can be illustrated by two minor episodes in the poet's own career. In 1696 Dryden's son, John Jr., published a play, *The Husband His Own Cuckold,* which was dedicated to his uncle Robert Howard and to which his father contributed a preface, an epilogue, and presumably the following motto from Virgil: "Et pater Aeneas et avunculus excitet Hector" (*Aeneid,* III, 343), a motto which may be freely rendered as "Let both his father Aeneas and his Uncle Hector spur him on to fame." [4] Some fifteen years earlier, in his first great satiric poem, Dryden had made effective use of the same line as model for a couplet suggesting the origins of Shadwell's incompetence in two earlier poetasters, his symbolic forebears; one of these addresses him as follows:

2. Knight, *Pope and the Heroic Tradition,* p. 52; cf. also pp. 74-5 and ch. ii, *passim.*

3. The difference in mixture reflects a difference in theme. *Mac Flecknoe* and *The Dunciad* present their protagonists, Shadwell and Cibber, as actively destructive forces of dullness and darkness, as direct contrasts to the light kindled in antiquity. Belinda and the Baron, on the other hand, act upon motives (fame, sexual desire) parallel to those of Homer's gods and heroes, though parallel at a considerable distance.

4. In the *Aeneid* the words, which Dryden has slightly modified, are spoken by Andromache concerning Aeneas' son Ascanius during an episode of the hero's wanderings toward Italy.

Let father Flecknoe fire thy mind with
            praise,
And uncle Ogilby thy envy raise.
                            (*Mac Flecknoe*, 173–4)

Virgilian rhetoric, evidently, was a weapon ever ready at hand, and a
weapon possessing a double-barreled effect. Used with a degree of self-
deprecating irony left evidently to the reader to determine, it could ele-
vate two of the lettered interlocutors of *An Essay of Dramatic Poesy*,
Dryden and Howard, to a rank in their culture like that of mythic
Trojans in theirs; or, translated and transmuted, it could consign the
less fortunate, Flecknoe and Ogilby, to a comic hell of alliterative
obloquy.

1. *The Mock Heroic: Homer, Juvenal, Virgil, Chaucer*

A sense of such double possibilities—at times, indeed, almost a waver-
ing between them—affected Dryden's translations, both for good and ill.
Such effect was inevitable because of the attitudes just described as characteristic of Dryden's period; because of the nature of his originals,
which were often either heroic or mock heroic themselves; and finally
because of the translating process itself, which, as we have seen in Chapter II, necessarily involves an adjustment of connotations and attitudes,
a constant manipulation of local symbolism, in accordance with the
translator's sense of what should be the total effect of his poem.

Nowhere can this adjustment of tone be more strikingly illustrated
than in the contrast between Dryden's and Pope's treatment of Homer's
Iliad, a contrast which also illustrates the two possible attitudes, just
discussed, which the enlightenment most often took toward the heroic.
The impression Homer made on Dryden can be inferred from two remarks, one made in the preface of his *Fables*, the other in the preface to
his *Examen Poeticum;* and each betrays a significant ambivalence of
feeling:

The chief talent of Virgil was propriety of thoughts, and ornament of
words: Homer was rapid in his thoughts, and took all the liberties,
both of numbers and of expressions, which his language, and the age
in which he lived, allowed him.

Homer . . . can move rage better than he can pity. He stirs up the
irascible appetite, as our philosophers call it; he provokes to murder,
and the destruction of God's images; he forms and equips those un-
godly man-killers, whom we poets, when we flatter them, call heroes;
a race of men who can never enjoy quiet in themselves, till they have
taken it from all the world. This is Homer's commendation; and, such

as it is, the lovers of peace, or at least of more moderate heroism, will never envy him.[5]

It thus came about that when Dryden, in the last year of his life and with the translation of the *Aeneid* his most recent poetical labor, embarked on an experimental rendering of the first book of the *Iliad,* what he produced was in mock-heroic vein, and in a mock-heroic vein, moreover, closer to that of *Hudibras* than to that of *The Rape of the Lock.* It also thus came about that when Pope, some fifteen years later, sat down to translate the same Greek, he found Dryden's Virgil—which he called "the most noble and spirited translation I know in any language" [6]—a far safer model than Dryden's labors in the same Homeric vineyard as his own. Where the two versions of Homer, Dryden's and Pope's, are closest together, they are often furthest apart, as in the following reference to Jove:

> *Dryden:* Embrace his knees, and at his footstool fall.
> (1, 562)
> *Pope:*   Embrace his knees, at his tribunal fall.
> (1, 531)

Dryden's deities are, in fact, the lusty inhabitants of a kind of perpetual Olympian alehouse, whose walls re-echo with salty personal invective or loud roars of drunken mirth; Pope, who "developed heroic morality beyond the Greek," [7] perhaps envisioned the relationships among Jove, the other Olympians, and mankind as somewhat analogous to those among God, the angels, and Adam and Eve in *Paradise Lost.* Dryden's Juno repulsed by his Jove sulks like a neglected spouse in a Restoration farce:

> One gracious word is for a wife too much:
> Such is a marriage vow, and Jove's own
>   faith is such.
> (1, 731–2)

whereas the conjugal relationship, in Pope's version, has been almost totally sublimated:

> Thy Juno knows not the decree of Fate,
> In vain the partner of imperial state.
> (1, 700–1)

5. *Essays,* ed. Ker, *2,* 251, 13–14.
6. *Complete Poetical Works of Alexander Pope,* ed. H. W. Boynton (Houghton Mifflin, 1903), p. 259. In the same paragraph of his preface to his *Iliad,* Pope gives guarded praise to Dryden's Homer, remarking that "if he has in some places not truly interpreted the sense, or preserved the antiquities" of the original, these lapses were doubtless due to haste, or to the influence of Chapman.
7. Knight, *Pope and the Heroic Tradition,* p. 99; cf. also p. 97 and the entire third chapter, "Tradition and Meaning."

Jove's reply, as rendered by each poet, is thoroughly appropriate to the two differing rebukes:

> *Dryden:* What I have hidden, hope not thou to know.
> Ev'n goddesses are women; and no wife
> Has pow'r to regulate her husband's life.
>
> (1, 734–6)

> *Pope:*   Seek not thou to find
> The sacred counsels of almighty mind.
> Involv'd in darkness lies the great decree,
> Nor can the depths of Fate be pierc'd by thee.
>
> (1, 704–7)

Similarly, when Jove rises from the sea in Pope's version he "Leads the long order of ethereal Powers" (1, 643); but in Dryden's, nautically enough, "A shoal of puny pow'rs attend his way" (1, 670).

Human life in Dryden's Homer exhibits a corresponding lack of dignity by contrast with the life of Pope's heroes,[8] though there are sometimes compensating gains. Alfred Tennyson commented,

> What a difference between Pope's little poisonous barbs and Dryden's strong invective! And how much more real poetic force is in Dryden:
> Look at Pope:
>   "He said, observant of the blue-eyed maid,
>   Then in the sheath return'd the shining blade."
> Then at Dryden:
>   "He said, with surly faith believ'd her word,
>   And in the sheath, reluctant, plung'd the
>   sword." [9]

In general, however, Dryden's Homer represents not only a change in tactics but a falling off in skill from his Virgil. That organizing talent which built up, in his *Aeneid,* the long metric paragraph full of poetic complexity was never sufficiently called into play in what he took to be the more primitive area of Homeric epic. We have only to compare his and Pope's versions of Achilles' oath,[1] the dramatic climax of *Iliad,* 1, to appreciate how much farther the organizing abilities present in Dryden but here only partly awake have been carried, at a critical point in the narrative, by his successor. Although Pope has fewer lines in his entire Book 1 than Dryden, he chooses here, at a dramatic crux, to extend Achilles' speech till it is one-and-one-half times as long, and several times as complex and unified, as it is in Dryden's version. No vigor of

---

8. At one point Pope's chiefs, asleep, "beside their vessel lie" (1, 622) while Dryden's "snore secure on decks till rosy morn" (1, 650).

9. Hallam Tennyson, *Alfred Lord Tennyson: A Memoir* (1897), 2, 287.

1. Dryden, 1, 348–57; Pope, 1, 309–24.

language at particular points can compensate in an epic for such a comparative failure as Dryden's in structural sense; and Homer was, moreover, of course less suited to the sort of treatment Dryden employed in *Iliad,* I, than were some of the other poets whom he translated.

One of these others was Juvenal; here methods analogous to those Dryden later used in his Homer bore excellent fruit. The fact that Juvenal's Latin is occasionally more elevated than Dryden's English, as for example in the following homely vignette from the Third Satire: [2]

> But he, for whom this busy care they take,
> Poor ghost, is wand'ring by the Stygian lake;
> Affrighted with the ferryman's grim face,
> New to the horrors of that uncouth place,
> His passage begs with unregarded pray'r,
> And wants two farthings to discharge his fare . . .
>
> (423–8)

makes little difference to the texture of satires which, in both Latin and English, are already a mixture of homespun and brocade. Indeed Dryden's commonplace diction, his unbuttoned ease of manner, in these satires, though, as we have already seen,[3] it resulted in less concentration of statement than Johnson later achieved while imitating the same poems, nevertheless was probably a positive advantage in dealing with Juvenal's obscenities, which fit more easily into an English poem whose style is already "low"—a fact which accounts for the translator's great force and pungency throughout the entire Sixth Satire. The passage [4] on the empress Messalina in that poem beginning

> The good old sluggard but began to snore,
> When from his side up rose th' imperial
> whore,

and concluding

> All filth without, and all a fire within,
> Tir'd with the toil, unsated with the sin,
> Old Caesar's bed the modest matron seeks . . .

is a remarkable example of Dryden's achievement in this genre. Throughout his satires occasional feminine rhymes, used I think oftener in the Juvenal than elsewhere in Dryden's translations, admirably contribute to the conversational tone:

2. For comment on the style of the Latin at this point, see I. G. Scott, *The Grand Style in the Satires of Juvenal* (Smith College, 1927), p. 50.
3. See above, pp. 56–8.
4. Ll. 163–89.

One happy hour is to a soldier better,
Than Mother Juno's recommending letter, . . .
(xvi, 6–7)

And 'tis the village mason's daily calling,
To keep the world's metropolis from falling.
(iii, 316–7)

When night-performance holds the place of
     merit,
And brawn and back the next of kin disherit.
(i, 55–6)

As we should expect from the nature of the mock heroic, Dryden's invective in his Juvenal generates its greatest power at the points where the spark gap between past and present, or between vulgar and heroic, is brought into operation. The following couplet has, I think, the authentic Drydenian ring, and would be recognized as his by any lover of *Absalom and Achitophel:*

From that old era whoring did begin,
So venerably ancient is the sin.
(vi, 30–1)

And the conclusion of the Sixth Satire offers a brilliant example.

Where'er you walk, the Belides you meet;
And Clytemnestras grow in every street.
But here's the difference; Agamemnon's wife
Was a gross butcher with a bloody knife;
But murther, now, is to perfection grown,
And subtle poisons are employ'd alone;
Unless some antidote prevents their arts,
And lines with balsam all the noble parts:
In such a case, reserv'd for such a need,
Rather than fail, the dagger does the deed.
(vi, 854–63)

In this passage, we start with the epic evocations of resounding classical proper names—the Belides and Clytemnestra; then the mood is abruptly punctured by the diction of the fourth line; finally the poetry returns to a high style, now charged with irony. In the last line, the general *content* of the crude fourth line is repeated, practically unchanged: "the dagger does the deed"; but the fine-sounding heroic connotations of "dagger" and "the deed" are now seen in the light of the gross butcher with the bloody knife.

If Dryden's Homer and Juvenal might be called examples of the gross mock heroic, parts of his Virgil and Chaucer offer a contrast: the elevated mock heroic. I refer specifically to the fourth Georgic and to "The Nun's Priest's Tale." In both of these the subject matter of the original is bucolic and indeed bestial in character; and in both the advantages of the English neoclassic style, for the achievement of light, glancing irony in a translation, are apparent.

In Dryden's version, the fourth Georgic begins as follows:

> The gifts of heav'n my foll'wing song pursues,
> Aërial honey, and ambrosial dews.
> Maecenas, read this other part, that sings
> Embattled squadrons, and advent'rous kings:
> A mighty pomp, tho' made of little things.
> Their arms, their arts, their manners, I
>   disclose,
> And how they war, and whence the people rose:
> Slight is the subject; but the praise not
>   small,
> If Heav'n assist, and Phoebus hear my call,
> First, for thy bees a quiet station find, . . .
>
> (IV, 1–10)

All kinds of parallelism, both within and between lines—between 2 and 4, for example—enhance the delicacy and shapeliness of the poetry and contribute to the muted epic tone ("Slight is the subject, but the praise not small,"—"Slight" and "small" being the operative words), the tone that forms an ironic background for the unadorned noun "bees" in line ten. The use of "heav'n" both for the regions in which the bees perform their operations and, capitalized, for the muse their poet invokes, gives the word a tinge of ambiguity admirably adapted to the vision of the bees as small and large at once, so to speak. Such a double vision, not unlike that presented by *The Rape of the Lock,* contrasts sharply with the attitude conveyed by the nineteenth-century Tennysonian translation of Lord Burghclere, a few lines of which follow:

> A wondrous drama of a pigmy world
> Citizens, soldiers, lords of high degree,
> And what their character, and what their
>   craft,
> A very nation with a nation's life
> In due array shall pass before thine eyes,
> Trivial the task but large the meed of
>   praise . . .[5]

---

5. *Georgics* (Murray, 1903), p. 149.

To Dryden the fact that the bees turn out to be much like men is not a matter for wonder, but for humor or irony.

In the description of the actual activities of the hive the same point about Dryden's special competence holds true. In the following passage from a recent rendering C. Day-Lewis (the translator) *says* that he is comparing small things with great, but his sociological diction divests the translation of irony:

> So, to compare small things
> With great, an inborn love of possession impels the
> bees
> Each to his own office. The old are the town's
> wardens,
> Who wall the honeycombs and frame the intricate
> houses.
> Tired, as night deepens, the young return from
> labour
> Their legs laden with thyme: . . .[6]

Dryden's version of the same passage runs:

> If little things with great we may compare,
> Such are the bees, and such their busy care;
> Studious of honey, each in his degree,
> The youthful swain, the grave, experienced bee:
> That in the field, this in affairs of state
> Employ'd at home, abides within the gate,
> To fortify the combs, to build the wall,
> To prop the ruins, lest the fabric fall:
> But, late at night, with weary pinions come
> The lab'ring youth, and heavy laden, home.
>
> (IV, 256–65)

The tone of the passage is a commentary on the content. The serious-seeming, rather elaborate phraseology—"Studious of honey," "the youthful swain," "weary pinions"—accords well with the serious pursuits of the bustling inhabitants, with their several "affairs of state." The verse itself is structurally elaborate and carefully worked out: thus the dichotomy between youth and age, announced in the parallelism of the fourth and fifth lines, is picked up again in the contrast between the last two couplets quoted. The only place (after the first couplet, which is connective and introductory) where the naked subject of all this delicate rhetoric is allowed to intrude is at the end of the fourth line, where

6. *Georgics of Virgil* (Cape, 1941), p. 82. The opening phrase refers to a preceding metaphor of the Cyclopes at their forges.

"bee" contrasts not only with its opposite number in the first half of the line ("swain") but also, and delightfully, with its own modifiers, "grave, experienced."

That Dryden's achievements in the genre of predominantly heroic mock-heroics were more a matter of re-creation than of translation in the most literal sense can be readily seen by comparison of his "The Cock and the Fox" with its original, Chaucer's "Nun's Priest's Tale." In the following passage, for example, which I quote first in the form in which Dryden read it in Speght's edition of Chaucer, then in his *Fables* version, the climactic phrase "widow'd poultry" (similar in effect to "grave, experienced bee") is entirely Dryden's own. The hens are lamenting Chanticleer's capture by the fox:

> Certes such cry ne lamentacion
> Nas never of Ladies made, whan that *Ilion*
> Was won, and *Pirrus* with his bright swerde
> Whan he hent King *Priam* by the berde,
> And slough him, (as saieth *Eneidos*)
> As made all the hennes in the cloos,
> Whan they had loste of Chaunticlere the
> sight: . . .
>
> (4545–51)

> Not louder cries, when Ilium was in flames,
> Were sent to heav'n by woful Trojan dames,
> When Pyrrhus toss'd on high his burnish'd blade,
> And offer'd Priam to his father's shade
> Than for the cock the widow'd poultry made.
>
> (699–703)

Much more is involved in such re-creation than simple changes of diction like "widow'd poultry" for "all the hennes." There is nothing intrinsically unheroic about "bright swerde," for example ("Keep up your bright swords, for the dew will rust them" was a line in *Othello* that Dryden must have known as well as we do); yet Dryden changes it to "burnish'd blade." What is involved is a complete reorganization of the passage, in the course of which images as well as language become transmuted. I should say that Chaucer's mock-heroic effect is concentrated chiefly in the contrast between the two line endings ". . . (as saieth Eneidos)" and ". . . the hennes in the cloos," by means of which he makes Virgil stalk the barnyard for an instant. Dryden gets the same sort of effect, more briefly, in "widow'd poultry," which he emphasizes (1) by placing it near the very end of a periodic sentence created by pushing "made" forward to the end of the last line quoted and bringing the loss of Chanticleer into the same line; (2) by anticipating the elegiac effect of "widow'd" in the "father's shade" image; and (3) by his couplet-plus-triplet structure, which more tightly links the elements of the passage and thus adds finality to "widow'd poultry" at the close of it. Tight linkage of this kind presupposes flexibility in the translating process: the noun "lamentacion" becomes the adjective "woful," and so forth.

A like degree of rearrangement, designed to emphasize parallelism, and therefore contrast, in line and couplet structure, occurs earlier in the same tale in the apostrophe to the wicked fox (I quote Robinson's text of Chaucer this time):

> O false mordrour, lurkynge in thy den!
> O newe Scariot, newe Genylon,
> False dissymulour, O Greek Synon,
> That broghtest Troye al outrely to sorwe!
> O Chauntecleer, acursed be that morwe
> That thou into that yerd flaugh fro the bemes!
>   (4416–21)

> O hypocrite, ingenious to destroy!
> O traitor, worse than Sinon was to Troy!
> O vile subverter of the Gallic reign,
> More false than Gano was to Charlemagne!
> O Chanticleer, in an unhappy hour
> Didst thou forsake the safety of thy bow'r . . .
>   (499–505)

Is it too much to say that the translator shows himself here a more skillful versifier than his distinguished forebear? If a modern prose version [7] is placed beside the two extracts just given:

> O, false murderer, lurking in thy lair! O second Iscariot! Second Ganilion! False dissimulator! O thou Greek Sinon, that broughtest Troy utterly to sorrow! O Chaunticleer, cursed be that morn that thou flewest from thy perch into that yard!

and if the degree to which rhythm, sound echoes, and arrangement of words play an organic role is examined for each of the three, then I think it must be said that Chaucer, in this passage, occupies a point somewhere between his two translators.

2. *The Heroic:* "PALAMON AND ARCITE"

Of all Dryden's translations in the purely heroic mode, except for his Virgil, "Palamon and Arcite," a version of Chaucer's "Knight's

7. P. MacKaye, *The Canterbury Tales: A Modern Rendering* (Fox, Duffield, 1904), p. 85.

Tale," is the most ambitious, the most energetic, and the most brilliant of execution. It is, however, only a partial success. On the level of versification it suffers from an occasional melodramatic, overly rhetorical quality that has drawn upon it the ire of such hostile writers as A. E. Housman; on the level of characterization, its principal weakness culminates in the deathbed speech of Arcite, one of its two protagonists, after he has won the tournament and the heroine, but suffered a fatal accident while leaving the field of contest. What is wrong with the deathbed speech has never been more clearly stated than by John Wilson ("Christopher North"), a warm admirer of Dryden's translations, in a comparison of "Palamon and Arcite" with its original, a comparison written about a century ago. Wilson comments as follows:

> Dryden, you observe, exhibits various changes. Are they for the better or the worse? In the first place, he introduces a new motive into the conduct of Arcite—remorse of conscience. When fate has declared against him, and he finds that he cannot enjoy the possession of the prize that he has wrongfully won, his eyes open upon his own injustice, and he acknowledges the prior right of Palamon, who had first seen Emilie . . . does it [this innovation] perplex the old heroic simplicity with a modern and needless refinement? . . . Really there seems to be something not only simpler in art, but more pathetic, and even morally greater, in the humble submission of the fierce and giant-like spirit to inevitable decree . . . and in his voluntarily appointing, so far as he ventures to appoint, his brother in arms and his bride to each other's happiness—than in the inventive display of a compunction for which, as the world goes, there appears to be positively no use, and hardly clear room . . .
>
> But that which, upon the general comparison of the two speeches, principally strikes us, is the great expansion, by the multiplying of the thoughts to which expression is given, by Dryden. With old Geoffrey, the weight of death seems actually to lie upon the tongue that speaks in few interrupted accents. Dryden's Moribund runs on, quite at his ease, in eloquent disquisition. . . . That mere cleaving desire to Emilie, felt through the first half in word after word gushing up from a heart in which life, but not love, ebbs, gets bewildered in the modern version among explications of the befallen unhappiness, and lost in a sort of argumentative lamentation.[8]

Wilson speaks here of Dryden's having introduced "a new motive into the conduct of Arcite—remorse of conscience" and of Arcite's finding that he cannot possess the prize he has "wrongfully won." Actually, the novelty is more drastic than a mere change of motive in Arcite at the conclusion of the tale; and the idea of Arcite's having *wrongfully* won

8. "Dryden and Chaucer," *Blackwood's Magazine*, 57 (1845), 781-2.

the hand of the heroine is one which the story owes chiefly to the translator. For without altering Chaucer's basic plot, Dryden has markedly shifted his central characters' interpretation of it.

The central ethical conflict in "The Knight's Tale" is between military comradeship and courtly love.[9] Palamon and Arcite, two young Theban knights, fall in love with Emily while imprisoned for life as a result of being captured in battle by Theseus, Duke of Athens and Emily's brother-in-law. Rivalry in love leads to a rupture in the friendship of the knights, a friendship which is only resumed when Arcite, having defeated Palamon in a tournament for Emily's hand, is dying as a result of an accidental fall from his horse sustained in the very moment of victory.

Within the framework of this basic plot, Chaucer presents the two knights with elaborate rhetorical parallelism in speeches and narrative, and with ostensible impartiality. A number of details concerning Arcite, however, come, in the light of the poem's conclusion, to be invested with possible symbolic overtones. Thus, Arcite falls in love with Emily after Palamon has, but brushes aside the former's prior right on the grounds that Palamon worships her as a goddess while he, Arcite, desires her as a woman; and that in matters of love, other loyalties are expendable. Later Arcite, having been released from prison by Theseus but banished for life from Athens, returns to that city in disguise to pursue a career at court incognito, while his rival still languishes behind bars. Later still, on the eve of the final tournament, Arcite prays to Mars for victory in battle, recalling in his prayer the god's adulterous pursuit of Venus; while Palamon, calling on Venus to remember her own devotion to Adonis, asks the goddess only for ultimate possession of Emily. These details suggest, it seems to me, that Arcite is to be regarded as the more practical minded and less idealistic of the two knights, being devoted to immediate ends and to devices of expediency, while Palamon is a "martyr" (Chaucer twice uses the term of him) to circumstances.

To Dryden such details evidently suggested a good deal more. "Chaucer," he says in his preface to the *Fables*,[1] "makes Arcite violent in his love, and unjust in the pursuit of it." Finding the moral inferiority of the second knight insufficiently clarified in his original, Dryden introduced certain touches—even extending to drastic changes in Chaucer's plain sense—into his translation, in accordance with his view of the values implicit in the story. To emphasize the violence of Arcite's passion, and no doubt also to foreshadow the knight's ultimate catastrophic fate, he translates Arcite's original declaration of love—

9. For a fuller discussion of the tale, see my "Interpretation of Chaucer's Knight's Tale," in *Review of English Studies*, 25 (1949), 289–304.

1. *Essays*, ed. Ker, 2, 257.

The fresshe beautee sleeth me sodeynly
Of hire that rometh in the yonder place—
(1118–19)

by the lurid ejaculation:[2]

The beauty I behold has struck me dead:
Unknowingly she strikes, and kills by chance;
Poison is in her eyes, and death in ev'ry glance . . .
(I, 277–9)

To emphasize the contrast in character between the two rivals, Dryden
translates Palamon's confession to Theseus—

I am thilke woful Palamoun
That hath thy prisoun broken wikkedly—
(1734–5)

by a speech in which he actually justifies his own escape, and compares
himself favorably with the perjured Arcite who has returned to Athens
in disguise:

Think me not like that man; since no disgrace
Can force me to renounce the honour of my race.
Know me for what I am: I broke thy chain,
Nor promis'd I thy pris'ner to remain:
The love of liberty with life is giv'n,
And life itself th' inferior gift of Heav'n.
Thus without crime I fled: . . .
(II, 287–93)

"Thus without crime I fled"—in the light of revisions as extensive and
methodical as these, it is no wonder that, as Wilson points out, Dryden
ultimately complicated Arcite's deathbed speech with a new motive—
remorse of conscience; the complication was thoroughly in keeping with
his previous methods of translating the tale.

As to why he employed such methods on this occasion we may speculate; and speculate, I think, with some hope of a definite answer. The
speech just quoted contains a clue, in the eloquent couplet on liberty.
"Palamon and Arcite" was the first translation printed in the *Fables*
volume of 1700, the volume being dedicated to the Duke of Ormond,
and the poem to his duchess. Ormond's political sympathies may be inferred from the loyalty of his grandfather, Barzillai in *Absalom and
Achitophel,* to Charles II, both before and after that monarch's restoration; and from his own later exile as a Jacobite, after the accession of

2. Cf. also Chaucer, l. 1542, with Dryden's triplet, II, 89–91; and Chaucer, l. 1364, with
Dryden's couplet, I, 528–9.

George I. In a dedicatory verse epistle of much wit and beauty prefixed to "Palamon and Arcite" Dryden associates his two noble patrons with specific characters in the poem, finding "A Palamon in him, in you an Emily."

All the evidence—more of which I shall cite in a moment—seems to me to suggest that Dryden, like Milton writing *Samson Agonistes* in his old age, projected into the symbolic situations of poetry emotions arising out of his own position in life and out of what he took to be the deteriorating political situation around him. Just as for Milton Dagon no doubt represented an analogue to the Anglican establishment, and Samson "eyeless in Gaza at the mill with slaves" a parallel to his own misfortunes and disabilities, so to Dryden the munificent Theseus, disregarding the enormous cost of temples and stadium for the tournament, formed a contrast to the monarchy which had deprived of his laureateship the chief—almost the only—poet of the age:

> So princes now their poets should regard;
> But few can write, and fewer can reward.
>
> (II, 661–2)

By a similar process Arcite became a symbol of military success vitiated by personal disloyalty (William III was an able soldier, and had ousted his predecessor James with little trouble); while Palamon represented loyal failure eventually rewarded by divine intervention.

Such feelings, in Dryden's translation, color especially the picture of Arcite in his moment of triumph, just after the tournament. In the following passage the reference to the standing army links Arcite and William III, and the fourth line quoted was, appropriately enough, applied to William directly when Pope later adapted it for use in a famous autobiographical passage of his satires: [3]

> Arcite is own'd by ev'n the gods above,
> And conqu'ring Mars insults the Queen of Love:
> So laugh'd he, when the rightful Titan fail'd,
> And Jove's usurping arms in heav'n prevail'd.
> Laugh'd all the pow'rs who favor tyranny;
> And all the standing army of the sky.
>
> (III, 667–72)

A few lines further on Arcite's manner as a victor is satirized (only the first line here owes anything to Chaucer):

> The victor knight had laid his helm aside,
> Part for his ease, the greater part for pride.

3. See his "Second Epistle of the Second Book of Horace":

"Hopes after hopes of pious papists fail'd,
While mighty William's thund'ring arm prevail'd" (ll. 62–3).

Bareheaded, popularly low he bow'd,
And paid the salutations of the crowd; . . .

(III, 687–90)

Here the second couplet contains a reminiscence of *Absalom and Achitophel* (of Absalom "bowing popularly low," 689); and consequently links Arcite with the disloyal demagogue Monmouth. Arcite's triumph —in Dryden, not in Chaucer—is, finally, reproved implicitly by Theseus, who makes the following generalizations to console the losers in the tournament:

If crowds and palms the conqu'ring side adorn,
The victor under better stars was born:
The brave man seeks not popular applause,
Nor, overpow'r'd with arms, deserts his cause;
Unsham'd, tho' foil'd, he does the best he can;
Force is of brutes, but honor is of man.

(III, 737–42)

If it be argued that changes such as I have been describing amount to no more than a difference of emphasis as between original and translation, it remains true that as a result of this different emphasis a certain delicacy of symbolism, economy of means, or artistic detachment, present in Chaucer, has been coarsened or weakened in Dryden's series of variations on the same themes. Chaucer's Arcite, though ambitious, is never arrogant; his Palamon, though reproachful, is never recriminatory. In Dryden the episode, illustrative of chivalry, in which Arcite returns to the city to provide arms and sustenance for the fugitive Palamon so that they may fight a private duel in the woods gives rise to a bickering sort of interchange between the knights that risks alienating the reader's sympathy from either (I italicize the innovations):

"And, that at better ease thou may'st abide,
Bedding and clothes I will this night provide,
And needful sustenance, *that thou may'st be*
A conquest better won, and worthy me."
His promise Palamon accepts; but pray'd,
To keep it better than the first he made.

(II, 158–63)

What I have said so far will give a misleading impression of "Palamon and Arcite," however, unless another point is immediately added. If the central idea of the tale in Chaucer were to present a comparison or contrast in personality of the rivals for Emily's hand, then Dryden's manipulation of that comparison might well be considered irretrievably damaging to his translation; but the interests of the tale are much broader than the view of them taken so far. The rivalry between the knights, which in the hands of a modern novelist would no doubt be the focus and center of the story, is actually, in Chaucer, largely incidental to such wider concerns as the general view of human environment and human destiny, a view epitomized in the figures of Theseus and Emily; in the symbolism associated with Mars, Venus, Saturn, and Diana; and in the reflective or philosophical speeches of several of the characters. In handling all these matters Dryden shows a versatility and resourcefulness certainly unsurpassed in other modernizers of Chaucer, and well calculated to create a series of heroic symbols in modern verse.

The figure of Theseus, who dominates the tale from beginning to end, forms, on the human level, an embodiment of destiny whose decisive qualities are well caught by the energy and rapidity of Dryden's transcription:

> *Chaucer:* He conquered al the regne of Femenye
> That whilome was ycleped Scithia,
> And weddede the queene Ypolita,
> And broghte hire hoom with hym in
> his contree
> With muchel glorie and greet solempnytee,
> And eek hir yonge suster Emelye.
> (866–71)

> *Dryden:* In Scythia with the warrior queen he
> strove,
> Whom first by force he conquer'd, then
> by love;
> He brought in triumph back the beauteous
> dame,
> With whom her sister, fair Emilia, came.
> (1, 7–10)

"Femenye" is important to Chaucer's story because Theseus represents success in the two kinds of endeavor the younger knights ultimately have to choose between: love and war. Dryden omits the name of the nation, but makes the same point by the antitheses in the second line quoted.

Emelye, or fair Emilia, is, like Theseus, mainly of importance as symbol; individualizing questions of personality are carefully excluded from her presentation. She is associated with May—"Fresh as the month, and as the morning fair" are Dryden's words about her; and the translator, in his additions to the details given in the original, preserves the atmosphere suggested by Chaucer with admirable delicacy. The following lines, for example, are entirely of Dryden's inspiration:

> At ev'ry turn she made a little stand,
> And thrust among the thorns her lily hand
> To draw the rose, and ev'ry rose she drew,
> She shook the stalk, and brush'd away the dew; . . .
>
> (I, 191–4)

The heroine's "turns" on her walk through the garden are reflected in the rhetorical turns of the poetry ("draw . . . drew").

Elsewhere I have already quoted passages illustrating Dryden's handling of the temples in "The Knight's Tale," and of Theseus as a military figure.[4] Throughout the tale, Chaucer's sense of the precariousness of the human situation—a perception essential to the existence of a heroic view of life—finds ready and convincing echoes in Dryden's rendition.

> Vain men, how vanishing a bliss we crave,
> Now warm in love, now with 'ring in the grave!
>
> (III, 796–7)

may be a sophistication of the more famous

> What is this world? what asketh men to have?
> Now with his love, now in his colde grave
> Allone, withouten any compaignye—;
>
> (2777–9)

but it is at least an eloquent one. The climax of the tale comes in Theseus' speech ending the period of mourning for Arcite and justifying the newly proposed marriage of Palamon and Emily; one of the great philosophical passages of Chaucerian poetry, this speech became in Dryden one of the finest of the seventeenth century, its Boethean vigor and loftiness undiminished in his transcription. Always a master at ideological poetry, he seizes on Chaucer's images, enlarges, contracts, rearranges, but preserves their spirit and their implications. The following is characteristic:

> *Chaucer:* Lo the ook, that hath so long a norisshynge
> From tyme that it first bigynneth to sprynge,
> And hath so long a lif, as we may see,
> Yet at the laste wasted is the tree.
> Considereth eek how that the harde stoon
> Under oure feet, on which we trede and goon,
> Yet wasteth it as it lyth by the weye.
> The brode ryver somtyme wexeth dreye;
> The grete tounes se we wane and wende
> Thanne may ye se that al this thyng hath ende.
>
> (3017–26)

4. See above, Ch. iii, pp. 45–7, 51, 61.

Dryden: The monarch oak, the patriarch of the trees,
Shoots rising up, and spreads by slow degrees;
Three centuries he grows, and three he stays,
Supreme in state, and in three more decays:
So wears the paving pebble in the street,
And towns and tow'rs their fatal periods meet;
So rivers, rapid once, now naked lie,
Forsaken of their springs, and leave their
channels dry.

(1058–65)

"The grete tounes se we wane and wende"—"And towns and tow'rs their fatal periods meet"—there is no question that, however unliteral the details of the translation, Dryden was surely correct in claiming a kinship between Chaucer's spirit and his own.

By way of postscript it may be added that, in one inevitable respect not yet mentioned, the spirit of "The Knight's Tale" differs from the spirit of "Palamon and Arcite": both are at times ironic, but in different ways. Chaucer's irony is sly, and presupposes the fiction of a relatively naïve narrator, the Knight of the Prologue to *The Canterbury Tales*. This narrator is sometimes the object of a gentle irony, as when he solemnly avers that women whose husbands die ordinarily follow them to the grave, an assurance Dryden blandly reverses in the translation;[5] and he is sometimes made to deprecate his own story-telling powers, as when he repeatedly states that he will say nothing about ceremonial details which he then proceeds to enumerate with hurried prolixity—a device of satire Dryden blurs in the translation.[6] Such matters, in Chaucer, enhance the sense of the tale's context, the general framework of the Canterbury collection, and give it an artistic distancing not open to Dryden, who was translating the tale as a self-contained unit only. What detachment Dryden has—and as we have seen, in the case of the character of Arcite he was perhaps not detached enough—comes from his occasionally developing a hint in Chaucer into a full-fledged Ovidian conceit. Arcite's funeral pyre, in the following passage, is being located on the very site where he had battled Palamon for Emily's hand:

Chaucer: That in that selve grove, swoote and
grene,

5. Cf. Chaucer, ll. 2820–6, a passage which concludes "at the laste certeinly they dye"; and Dryden's corresponding III, 860–4, ending with couplet:

"But like a low-hung cloud, it rains so fast,
That all at once it falls, and cannot last"—

it being a widow's grief!

6. Cf. the handling of the catalogues of trees at Arcite's funeral: Chaucer, ll. 2919 ff.; Dryden, III, 959 ff. See above, Ch. iii, pp. 36–8.

Ther as he hadde his amorouse desires,
His compleynte, and for love his hoote
fires,
He wolde make a fyr in which the office
Funeral he myghte al accomplice.

(2860–4)

Dryden: That, where he fed his amorous desires
With soft complaints, and felt his
hottest fires,
There other flames might waste his
earthly part,
And burn his limbs, where love had
burn'd his heart.

(III, 900–3)

3. *The Heroic:* THE AENEID

I have already mentioned, in Chapter III, Dryden's occasional use of a Latinate idiom in his Virgil translations as imparting a "period" flavor to his style, and as being addressed perhaps especially to the educated reader. Besides their appeal to certain readers of the seventeenth century, such features of Dryden's style are symptomatic of one of his greatest qualifications not only as a translator but even as a reader of the *Aeneid:* the fact that to him Latin was a living language, maintaining a living relationship to English. Its buried metaphors were, for him, buried only just beneath the surface, and ripe for resurrection. Similarly, its many derivatives in English were likely to be alive with their original and their derived suggestiveness simultaneously. This sense of the vitality of Virgil's language, and the potential extra vitality of his own English in relation to Virgil's, made for the greatest possible flexibility in Dryden's rendering of any given passage in the *Aeneid*.

Take, for example, the carving of Pasiphae by Dedalus, at the opening of Book VI. Dedalus, the craftsman who devised the imitation cow encased in which Pasiphae mated with the bull and conceived the Minotaur, is represented by Virgil as having commemorated this episode of his past by carvings on the door of the temple of Apollo at Cumae, where Aeneas disembarked to consult the Sibyl. The Latin runs:

hic crudelis amor tauri, suppostaque furto
Pasiphaë, mixtumque genus prolesque biformis
Minotaurus inest, Veneris monumenta nefandae.

(VI, 24–6)

Dryden translates:

There too, in living sculpture, might be seen
The mad affection of the Cretan queen;
Then how she cheats her bellowing lover's eye;
The rushing leap, the doubtful progeny,
The lower part a beast, a man above,
The monument of their polluted love.

(VI, 33–8)

"Doubtful" because "misceo," the verb from which "mixtum" comes, can mean both "to mingle" and "to confuse." "The rushing leap" because "supposta," besides meaning "substituted" (hence "cheats . . . eye"), also means "placed beneath" ("sub" plus "posita"), and therefore evokes a sexual stress in the translation. "Monument" because this translation of the Latin fits not only, with irony, the grotesque Minotaur; but also, in a literal sense, Dedalus' "living sculpture" at Cumae: not only the Minotaur, but the mating, is a monument of the polluted love. This last suggestion cannot be given by a mere *translation* of "monumenta," such as Humphries' "proof," T. C. Williams' "sign," or Day-Lewis' "memento." "Virgil has a thousand secret beauties," wrote Dryden in his introductory dedication of the *Aeneid* to the Marquis of Normanby; and the instance he gives is the effect on Dido of Aeneas' narrative concerning the risks he ran in vainly trying to rescue his wife from burning Troy: "That he had been so affectionate a husband was no ill argument to the coming dowager that he might prove as kind to her." It was this sort of awareness of the context of each episode in its framework that led him to use "monument" to put the Pasiphae story back into the sculpture Aeneas saw.

What then was the nature of the total context within which Dryden translated each passage of his *Aeneid?*

Virgil's *Aeneid,* it seems to me, can most easily be discussed by means of a brief comparison to Homer's *Odyssey,* on which it is—at least in the crucial first six books—obviously based as a poem. Each epic presents various contrasts between order and chaos. Order, in the *Odyssey,* includes pre-eminently the ideal, divinely graced, kingdom of the Phaeacians; but also the figure of the royally born swineherd Eumaeus, who befriends Odysseus after he arrives in Ithaca; and, in the four opening books which describe the expedition of Odysseus' son Telemachus, the stable courts and kingdoms of Nestor and Menelaus. Chaos is represented pre-eminently by the ocean abroad and suitors at home, the ocean always threatening to swallow up Odysseus and his comrades, the suitors consuming his substance in riotous disorder and making a mockery of the political management of Ithaca. Chaos also takes the form of the individualistic and primitive Cyclopes (under the special protection of Poseidon, god of the sea); of the various distractions and dangers on the journey (the lotus-eaters and Circean enchantments, for example, which suggest failures of morale) ; and of the fate of Agamemnon, murdered in his own home by his treacherous wife.[7]

The order-chaos contrast, then, is partly domestic, partly political, partly physical and environmental, and partly religious. It is domestic in the contrast of the internal relationship of the Odysseus and Agamemnon family; political in such events as the disobedience of Odysseus' crew when they eat the Sun-cattle, or in the fidelity to Odysseus of Eumaeus; physical in its various images of a hostile or recalcitrant environment yielding to the ingenuity of man; and religious in its loving description of sacrifices and ceremonies, or in the vengeance visited on those who—like Aegisthus in seducing Agamemnon's wife, or like Odysseus in his boasting after he has outwitted the Cyclops Polyphemus—recklessly defy the gods. The physical and environmental images are particularly important and constant throughout the epic: the building of the raft for the escape from Ogygia; the violence of the storm which tears the shipwrecked Odysseus from the rocks he momentarily clings to, leaving bits of flesh torn from his hands on their surface; the elaborate and well-ordered hut of the swineherd, with its castle-like details, all constructed by Eumaeus himself; the rich gifts exchanged among rulers; the pastoral settings, and especially the garden of the Phaeacians; and certain scenes like the conclusion of Book v, where the wandering hero, tossed up on the Phaeacian coast more dead than alive, terrified of the cold, the wet, and the possible dangers from unknown wild animals, prepares a shelter for the night:

Not far from the river he found a copse with a clear space all round it. Here he crept under a pair of bushes, one an olive, the other a wild olive, which grew from the same stem with their branches so closely intertwined that when the winds blew moist not a breath could get inside, nor when the sun shone could his rays penetrate their shade, nor could the rain soak right through to the earth. Odysseus crawled into this shelter, and after all he had endured was delighted to see the ground littered with an abundance of dead leaves, enough to provide covering for two or three men in the·hardest winter weather. He set to work with his hands and scraped up a roomy couch, in the middle of which he lay down, and piled the leaves over himself, covering his body as carefully as a lonely crofter in the far corner of an estate

7. The whole Agamemnon story, including the revenge of Orestes, Agamemnon's son, seems particularly central and structural to the *Odyssey*, being brought in again and again; at the beginning of the poem, in the council in heaven; at the end, in the reception of the suitors in hell; in the middle, when the two warriors, Odysseus and Agamemnon, meet in the afterworld; and elsewhere. Telemachus is enjoined to model himself on the Hamlet-like Orestes; Odysseus ironically warned to distrust the exemplary Penelope; and the suitors implicitly likened to the adulterous Aegisthus, who had seduced Agamemnon's wife.

buries a gleaming brand under the black ashes to keep his fire alive and save himself from having to seek a light elsewhere. (Rieu's translation.)

Such a passage—there is nothing like it in the *Aeneid*—dramatizes unmistakably Homer's perception of the struggle on the part of human nature to make a characteristically human world; the image of the crofter and the fire gives the abnormal situation of Odysseus a relevance to everyday concerns. As Odysseus struggles on this exceptional occasion, so do remote ranch hands struggle in the ordinary course of their employment. The monstrous cannibalistic Cyclopes, in their brutal primitivism and lack of political or social cohesion, contrast with the hospitality, cosmopolitanism, and sensitiveness to public opinion of the gracious Phaeacian monarchy, the two races symbolizing opposite poles of civilization and barbarism. In the second book, the assembly in Ithaca is an image of political order in that it takes place at all, of disorder in respect to the cynical participation in it of the suitors.

In summary, it might be said that (from one point of view at least) the *Odyssey* is a poem about civilization itself, in the individual, the family, and the social group; about how it is achieved, what forces threaten it, and what maintaining it involves. Civilization is a simple absolute; it is noteworthy that the *Odyssey* does not envisage different *forms* of civilization existing in space, or any historical development of it in terms of history. When Odysseus, for example, tells Eumaeus a long cock-and-bull story of his exploits among the Egyptians he does not bother to color it with what we should think of as characteristically Egyptian details; the Egyptian king, he says, spared his life for fear of offending Zeus, the special god of strangers and suppliants. The Greeks in the *Odyssey* have no self-consciousness, no awareness of the peculiarly Greek nature of their art, or worship, or government. There is only civilization itself, and outside that the mysterious, the magic, the divine, the wild, the unpredictable—the capricious divinities and sub-divinities, the immeasurable, untamable ocean. Civilization rests squarely on a bedrock of nonhuman nature, and is achieved under conditions posited by superhuman gods; there are no intervening layers—except magical ones—of semicivilized, or differently civilized, cultures.

In this respect the *Aeneid* presents an important contrast. When Odysseus visited the underworld he had obtained information from the prophet Tiresias as to the conditions on which he could return home, be reunited with his family, and reassume the government of Ithaca. But when Aeneas, under similar circumstances, interviews the shade of his father Anchises, he is given a vision of the dynasty he will found in Italy, of the gradual growth of his nation to greatness, and of its eventual significance in world history:

Let others better mold the running mass
Of metals, and inform the breathing brass,
And soften into flesh a marble face;
Plead better at the bar; describe the skies,
And when the stars descend, and when they rise.
But Rome, 'tis thine alone, with awful sway,
To rule mankind, and make the world obey,
Disposing peace and war thy own majestic way;
To tame the proud, the fetter'd slave to free:
These are imperial arts, and worthy thee.
                    (Dryden's translation: vi, 1168–77)

Here the fine arts, the eloquence, and the science of Greece are ex-
plicitly distinguished from, and contrasted with, the peculiar destiny of
the new nation. And this destiny is seen not in relation to subhuman
strata of hostile environment and bestial primitivism but in relation to
other, alternative civilizations—such as the Greek and the Carthaginian
—which are presented as less responsible, and therefore unworthy of
world empire. Hence, if the *Odyssey* is about civilization in general, the
Aeneid might be said to be about a particular civilization.

In this respect Books II and IV are basic to the structure of the latter
epic. Each is centered around a city to which the hero has become at-
tached but which he is forced to leave—the first, Troy, because it is a
doomed and dying city; the second, Carthage, because it is simply a
foreign city, the wrong city. Book II presents a powerful series of images
of a civilization in process of disruption: the confusion, the night fight-
ing, the senseless brutality, the conflagrations, the repeated temptation
to return into the whirlpool, the fate of the civilian population, the destruction of buildings. The scene in which Aeneas and a small party of
Trojans, having disguised themselves in Greek uniforms and scored a
number of local successes by this means, lose their heads and attempt a
public rescue of a Trojan priestess, with the result that they are attacked
simultaneously by friend and foe (foes on the ground and friends on
the roofs), seems particularly symbolic of the degree of chaos which
is to explain and justify the imperial order to be established by Rome.
But it is not a form of chaos derived from the environment or from
pure barbarism: in the *Aeneid,* though the sea remains dangerous, Nep-
tune is on the hero's side, not against him; and Polyphemus the Cyclops represents no active threat to the wanderers. The chaos is instead
a cancerous growth—here, purely destructive warfare—on the body of
civilization itself, calling for the birth of a new and healthier—or at
least more stable—form and concept of civilization.

In Book IV, the threat to Aeneas' destiny is internal and psychological,
rather than external and military, though it is also connected with an

alternate city to Rome; here it takes the form of the triumph of the irrational in Dido's nature, leading to her suicide—a symbolic forecast of the ultimate fate of the rival Carthaginian empire, perhaps. By the conclusion of the episode, Dido has become a sinister figure, as her internal torments suggest to her a series of images of revenge on the Trojans; and the nightmare-like quality of all irrational threats to social order is one of the pervading motifs of the *Aeneid*.

To sum up, I should say that Homer encompasses a wider range of possible human experience than Virgil, and that this fact was at the root of the difficulties the English Augustan translators, Dryden and Pope, had in dealing with the *Iliad*. On the other hand, Virgil's characteristic themes, the psychological and sociological threats to social order, were precisely those which Dryden, in much of his original poetry, had already shown that he understood and could deal with brilliantly. *Absalom and Achitophel*, for example, embodies a dramatization of just such themes. It is the unfortunate modernity of the kinds of chaos or distortion Virgil embodied, for example in such personifications as his Rumour and his Allecto, that has helped, no doubt, to keep his epic alive into our own day. And perhaps one clue as to why Dryden succeeded better, by common consent, than all previous or subsequent translators of the *Aeneid* may be sought in lines from his greatest original poem, lines which Virgil himself would have had no difficulty in understanding:

> The sober part of Israel, free from stain,
> Well knew the value of a peaceful reign;
> And, looking backward with a wise affright,
> Saw seams of wounds, dishonest to the sight:
> In contemplation of whose ugly scars
> They curs'd the memory of civil wars.
>   (*Absalom and Achitophel*, 69–74)

Such may have been, at any rate, one reason for the appeal that Virgil, above all classical authors, had for Dryden in particular. As for the translator's failures and successes with the epic, I have already said a good deal, in Chapter II, about various local effects in the *Aeneid;* here I shall speak of certain emotional qualities perceptible, I think, in Virgil, and closely related to his central themes, as these appear to me. To sum up at the start of the discussion, I should say that Dryden is less intense than Virgil in communicating certain effects of horror and of pathos, but that in central situations dealing with the order-disorder conflict of the *Aeneid* he is at his best as a translator.

While discussing Dryden's line structure I have already instanced the following two translations of *Aeneid*, IV, 609: "*Nocturnisque Hecate triviis ululata per urbes*"—

Fairclough: And Hecate, whose name is shrieked by night at the crossroads of cities.

Dryden: Thou Hecate, hearken from thy dark abodes!

The passage is one in which Dido appeals to the eternal powers for vengeance upon her absconding lover; the context of the line in Dryden's translation runs:

> Thou Sun, who view'st at once the world below;
> Thou Juno, guardian of the nuptial vow;
> Thou Hecate, hearken from thy dark abodes!
> Ye Furies, fiends, and violated gods,
> All pow'rs invok'd with Dido's dying breath,
> Attend her curses and avenge her death!
>
> (872–7)

Probably the strongest element in this passage, a representative example of an emotional climax as handled by Dryden, is "violated gods" (there are no gods of any sort in the corresponding line of the Latin); by alliteration with "vows" and "invok'd" the chief meaning of the expression, that Aeneas has wantonly disregarded sacred obligations, is reinforced, but the other implication of the participle ("raped"), which suits well with the state of Dido's mind, cannot be excluded— it is almost as though Aeneas were being accused of felonious assault on the persons of Apollo, Hecate, and Juno themselves. The rest of the passage, with its obvious but vigorous sound echoes, and its ostensible parallelism leading to a sudden substitution of a verb for an appositive in the third line ("Thou Hecate, hearken . . ."), exhibits the usual Augustan balance, clarity, ease, and control, but is less remarkable as translation.

Indeed, in respect to the line concerning Hecate, excellent in its own way as a part of the total English curse, the translation shows an obvious inadequacy to Virgil. *Nocturnisque Hecate triviis ululata per urbes,* by a brilliant union of sound and sense, rises to a pitch of hysteria that the English does not even try to suggest. The "ees" rhymes, the unusual onomatopoetic verb "ululata," the staccato alliteration of t and k sounds, and above all the crowding of ideas in a tightly packed hexameter—I do not say that *any* translation can come near the total effect that Virgil has achieved here; only that Dryden's goes in a distinctly different direction. He is somber and dignified, melodramatic in "Furies, fiends," but not wrought up to the same pitch as Virgil.

In dealing with another emotional effect in the *Aeneid,* Dryden is perhaps more perceptive of what Virgil is about, but is also less restrained—even, one might say, cruder—than his original. The episode

with Dido is only one example, during the first six books, of Aeneas'
tendency to be deflected from his ultimate objective by a natural eager-
ness to re-establish Trojan civilization as quickly as possible, or at any
rate to find *some* sort of homeland, *somewhere,* in the course of his wanderings. This situation, which again is peculiarly Virgilian, gives rise
to the intense nostalgia of certain episodes, notably the one in which
Aeneas visits the former Trojan hero Helenus, who has meanwhile pros-
pered and established a kind of substitute Troy at Buthrotum, on the
west coast of Greece. Helenus has married Andromache, the widow of
Hector, Troy's chief hero; and Andromache, at the moment of parting
from Aeneas, who leaves to pursue his quest, is reminded by Aeneas'
son Ascanius of her own son Astyanax, who as an infant had figured in
one of the most famous scenes in the *Iliad*. She says:

> sic oculos, sic ille manus, sic ora ferebat;
> et nunc aequali tecum pubesceret aevo.
>
> (III, 490–1)

Dryden's version runs:

> Thou call'st my lost Astyanax to mind;
> In thee his features and his form I find:
> His eyes so sparkled with a lively flame;
> Such were his motions; such was all his frame;
> And ah! had Heav'n so pleas'd, his years had
>   been the same.
>
> (III, 632–6)

There seems to be no question here of Dryden's sensitivity to the
chief emotional and metrical effect of the Latin, the succession of heavy
spondees in the second of the two lines:

$$\overline{\text{et}} \ \overline{\text{nunc}} \ \overline{\text{aequali}} \ \overline{\text{tecum}} \ \overline{\text{pubesceret}} \ \overline{\text{aevo}}$$

(compare

> *which cost Ceres all that pain*
> To seek her through the world

from the field-of-Enna passage in *Paradise Lost,* IV). This lengthening
Dryden deliberately imitates in his triplet and alexandrine. One of the
main reasons, however, why the Latin is more moving than the English is precisely the fact that Virgil's Andromache does *not* say "And ah!
had Heav'n so pleas'd."

I do not want to imply that Dryden seems to me to sentimentalize or
vulgarize the speech fatally. It is a difficult passage to translate at all.
Opposite temptations can be illustrated in the Victorian version of T. C.
Williams, who yields to the lure of ejaculation:

—O thou that art
Of my Astyanax in all this world
The only image! His thy lovely eyes!
Thy hands, thy lips, are even what he bore,
And like thy own his youthful bloom would be.

and in the "tough" modern rendering of Rolfe Humphries, who throws overboard the metrical weight and the literal meaning of "pubesceret" at once:

your hands,
Your face, your eyes, remind me of him so,—
He would be just your age.

Dryden, I think, escapes both banal sentimentality and banal matter-of-factness; but he undeniably makes explicit what was implicit in the Latin, and his translation shows little compensatory strength of its own in this passage.

As for Dryden's strengths in his *Aeneid,* these come mainly, it seems to me, from his sympathetic understanding of the Roman ideals of civilization as embodied in epic verse; and from his aptness in finding adequate imagery and language to correspond to the many Virgilian versions of chaos.

Take for example the following pair of similes from Book VII. Aeneas has landed in Italy; Juno has succeeded in stirring up the inhabitants to make war upon him; and Virgil pauses to emphasize the innumerableness of the Italian native troops drawn up to fight the Trojans:

Quam multi Libyco volvuntur marmore fluctus
saevus ubi Orion hibernis conditur undis,
vel cum sole novo densae torrentur aristae
aut Hermi campo aut Lyciae flaventibus arvis
(VII, 717–20) [8]

The carefully arranged imagery dramatizes the immensity and formidableness of what the hero must overcome. Part of the interest of the passage comes from the number of contrasted ideas uniting to express a feeling of abundance. Thus we have Africa set against Asia (Libya: Lycia); the night against the day (Orion: the sun); the land against the sea (waves: harvests); and, above all, a rather dismal plenitude (*saevus Orion*) against a rich, inviting one (*densae aristae*). This basic structure in the imagery Dryden has readily comprehended in his translation—thus his "pale" though not a literal rendering of *saevus,* pre-

8. "as many as the waves that roll on the Libyan main, when fierce Orion sinks in the wintry waves; or thick as the corn-ears that are scorched by the early sun in the plains of Hermus or the yellow fields of Lycia"—Fairclough, *Virgil* . . . (Putnam, 1922). For T. C. Williams, see his *Aeneid of Virgil* (Houghton Mifflin, 1908).

serves the Virgilian contrast of the repellent winter seascape and the rich summer uplands:

> Not thicker billows beat the Libyan main,
> When pale Orion sets in wintry rain;
> Nor thicker harvests on rich Hermus rise,
> Or Lycian fields, when Phoebus burns the skies,
> Than stand these troops . . .
>
> (VII, 994–8)

Beneath the contrast, in both original and translation, lies a deeper basis of unity; both sets of images are being used to bring out something about the Italian troops. Like the billows, they are a sinister force, an unfavorable and destructive natural element which the voyaging Trojans have still to oppose before the City can be founded. Like the harvest, they must be reaped by Aeneas before the historic fertility of the new-found land can pass into his keeping. When we compare Dryden's translation with a more recent one:

> they came like waves
> Rolling to Africa's coast when fierce Orion
> Sinks in the wintry ocean, as thick as grain
> Turned brown in early summer on Hermus' plain
> Or Lydia's yellow acres.
>
> (Humphries, p. 202)

we may notice the force of Dryden's active verbs: "beats . . . sets . . . rise . . . burns . . . stand"; and the contrast in Dryden's heavens between Orion and Phoebus, a contrast that perhaps suggests the Turnus-Aeneas figures who are to be the heroes of the last six books. Both translations are musical, and deftly arranged to bring out the Virgilian parallels; only Dryden's, however, communicates the sense of activity essential to an epic, and especially to a Roman one.

Dryden's sensitivity to the peculiarly Roman nature of the *Aeneid* comes out well in a passage I have already quoted, the words of Anchises to Aeneas in the underworld. Part of it goes, in Latin and English, as follows:

> Excudent alii spirantia mollius aera,
> credo equidem, vivos ducent de marmore voltus,
> orabunt causas melius, caelique meatus
> describent radio, et surgentia sidera dicent:
> tu regere imperio populos, Romane, memento . . .
>
> (VI, 847–51)

> Let others better mold the running mass
> Of metals, and inform the breathing brass,

And soften into flesh a marble face;
Plead better at the bar; describe the skies,
And when the stars descend, and when they rise.
But Rome, 'tis thine alone, with awful sway,
To rule mankind. . . .

(vi, 1168–74)

The main feature of the translation is the extension of the sculpture imagery. A modern editor comments that Virgil's *ducent* "applies strictly to yielding materials, like metal, clay, or wax; its use here suggests that marble itself is pliable in the hands of a consummate artist . . ."[9] Dryden may well have been trying to echo this special effect of *ducent* by his "soften into flesh," a similar stretching of imagery. What is most striking about his translation, I think, is its suggestion of *parallels,* rather than merely contrasts, between the "others" (i.e., the Greeks) and the Romans; molding liquid metals, infusing form into brass, and softening marble faces are ways of giving form to chaos, and humanity to bureaucratic machinery.

I shall take my two final examples from passages that have been objected to, in Dryden's Virgil, as not sufficiently literal, or as embodying a fault of style. Here is Aeneas, his fleet seemingly about to be destroyed by a storm, regretting that he had not died, more nobly, in the defense of Troy. I italicize certain expressions that have no basis in the Latin:

Struck with unusual fright, the Trojan chief,
With lifted hands and eyes, invokes relief;
And, "Thrice and four times happy those," he
cried,
"That under Ilian walls before their parents died!
Tydides, bravest of the Grecian train!
Why could not I by that strong arm be slain,
And lie by noble Hector on the plain,
Or great Sarpedon, in those bloody fields
Where Simois rolls the bodies and the shields
Of heroes, *whose dismember'd hands yet bear
The dart aloft, and clench the pointed spear!*"

(i, 135–45)

The hands may be merely thrust by their possessors above the river water for a second or they may have been literally "dismember'd" in battle. Dryden's sense of chaos has weirdly enriched the imagery of the Latin original, and has added an overtone springing from Aeneas' situation; for the Trojan chief's own hands are at this moment lifted—in prayer. Virgil had him think of his native Simois as a better place to

9. J. B. Greenough and C. L. Kittredge, *Greater Poems of Virgil* (1900), *1,* 393.

drown in than the trackless Mediterranean; Dryden has him also projecting himself, heroic task unfulfilled, into the imagined moment of ignominious submersion.

Six books later, after many adventures, the hero arrives in Latium and appeals to King Latinus for help, describing in the course of the appeal his past misfortunes: the fall of his homeland, Troy; and his subsequent wandering at sea. To the following couplets, summarizing this description, Dryden contributed, most notably, an adjective, "frozen," and a periphrasis, "the wat'ry waste":

> How dire a tempest, from Mycenae pour'd,
> Our plains, our temple, and our town devour'd;
> What was the waste of war, what fierce alarms
> Shook Asia's crown with European arms;
> Ev'n such have heard, if any such there be,
> Whose earth is bounded by the frozen sea;
> And such as, born beneath the burning sky
> And sultry sun, betwixt the tropics lie.
> From that dire deluge, thro' the wat'ry waste,
> (Such length of years, such various perils past,)
> At length escap'd, to Latium we repair, . . .
>
> (VII, 302–12)

"Wat'ry waste," as a periphrasis, derives force not only from the specific circumstances of Aeneas here but also from the poetic devices of the entire passage. "Waste" is the theme of these half-dozen couplets; Aeneas' mind is seeing the world in terms of "waste." In the first two lines we are given an epitome of the "waste of war," which is thought of in terms of a metaphorical flood or tempest pouring from Mycenae, the home city of Helen of Troy, in revenge for her elopement with Paris. This tempest metaphor is reiterated in line 9: "From that dire deluge . . ." Thus the outcasts move from a war as destructive as a flood to the flood of ocean itself, "the wat'ry waste"; and the yoking of the two waters in one line ("From that dire deluge, thro' the wat'ry waste") creates the effect of a vast desolate experience, pervading and shaping the whole passage. Even the two couplets about the widespread fame of the war ("Ev'n such have heard," etc.), lines which logically have no necessary connection with the fall of Troy or the later wanderings, are yet made to embody, in Dryden's version, two more wastes: the glacial arctic deserts and the arid Saharas of the tropics.

V

Conclusion

ACCORDING to recent critical theory,[1] the best poetry of the English Augustan age was that which implicitly repudiated the announced Augustan literary ideals—clarity, distinctness, reason, order—in order to celebrate a kind of surrealistic vision, an "infra-reality"—chiefly, of course, in satire. This theory draws a line between "official" Augustan poetry and "play" poetry; between tenuous diagrams of a too facile world harmony, and richly complex realizations of chaos or evil. According to such a theory, it would be easy to "place" the chief among the more heroic seventeenth-century translations in respect to, and in inferior relation to, the satire of that and the succeeding age. Thus we may juxtapose two priest kings, Helenus and Flecknoe, in moments of prophecy:

> The prophet first with sacrifice adores
> The greater gods; their pardon then implores;
> Unbinds the fillet from his holy head;
> To Phoebus, next, my trembling steps he led,
> Full of religious doubts and awful dread.
> Then, with his god possess'd, before the shrine,
> These words proceeded from his mouth divine: . . .
> (Dryden's *Aeneid,* III, 473–9)

> The sire then shook the honors of his head,
> And from his brows damps of oblivion shed
> Full on the filial dullness: long he stood,
> Repelling from his breast the raging god;
> At length burst out in this prophetic mood: . . .
> (*Mac Flecknoe,* 134–8)

Or two visions of the afterlife:

> The chief beheld their chariots from afar,
> Their shining arms, and coursers train'd to war:
> Their lances fix'd in earth, their steeds around,
> Free from their harness, graze the flow'ry ground.

1. W. K. Wimsatt, Jr., "The Augustan Mode in English Poetry," *ELH, 20* (1953), 1–14; cf. also the materials cited by Wimsatt, especially Austin Warren's "The Mask of Pope," from his *Rage for Order* (Univ. of Chicago Press, 1948).

The love of horses which they had, alive,
And care of chariots, after death survive.
(Dryden's Aeneid, VI, 885–90)

Think not, when Woman's transient breath is fled,
That all her vanities at once are dead;
Succeeding vanities she still regards,
And though she plays no more, o'erlooks the cards.
Her joy in gilded chariots, when alive,
And love of Ombre, after death survive.
(Rape of the Lock, Canto i, 51–6)

Or two resurrection symbols:

And he said unto me, Son of man, can these bones live? And I
answered, O Lord God, thou knowest.
(1611 Bible, Ezekiel 37:3)

Can dry bones live? or skeletons produce
The vital warmth of cuckoldizing juice?
(Absalom and Achitophel, II, 338–9)

My main objection to the foregoing neat schematization of the poetic
impulses of Dryden's age is that, in respect to the heroic mode, it runs a
risk of throwing out the baby with the bath. In the heroic-burlesque seesaw constructed by the advocates of the "official poetry"–"play poetry"
theory, the weightier end of the beam seems to be too invariably, and too
heavily, occupied by the burlesque. By extending the period under consideration both forward and backward in time a little, it is possible to
make the seesaw—as the last example above suggests—tilt a bit in the
other direction:

O now for ever

Farewell the tranquil mind! farewell content!
Farewell the plumed troops and the big wars
That make ambition virtue! O farewell,
Farewell the neighing steed and the shrill trump,
The spirit-stirring drum, th' ear-piercing fife,
The royal banner, and all quality,
Pride, pomp, and circumstance of glorious war!
And O you mortal engines whose rude throats
Th' immortal Jove's dread clamors counterfeit,
Farewell! Othello's occupation's gone!
(Othello, III, iii, 347–57)

The transient hour of fashion too soon spent,
Farewell the tranquil mind, farewell content!

Farewell the plumèd head, the cushion'd tête,
That takes the cushion from its proper seat!
That spirit-stirring drum!—card drums I mean,
Spadille—odd trick—pam—basto—king and queen!
And you, ye knockers, that, with brazen throat,
The welcome visitors' approach denote;
Farewell all quality of high renown,
Pride, pomp, and circumstance of glorious town!
Farewell! your revels I partake no more,
And Lady Teazle's occupation's o'er!
(Epilogue to *The School for Scandal*)

Even within the Augustan age proper, it is perhaps too large an assumption that the Elizabethan heroic sunset has wholly faded to insipid pastel. The following parallel, for example, suggests something other than degeneration:

The knight much wondred at his suddeine wit,
And sayd: "The terme of life is limited,
Ne may a man prolong, nor shorten it:
The souldier may not move from watchfull sted,
Nor leave his stand, untill his captaine bed."
(*Faerie Queene*, I, Canto ix, 41)

Brutus and Cato might discharge their souls
And give 'em furloughs for another world;
But we like sentries are obliged to stand
In starless nights, and wait the pointed hour.
(Dryden, *Don Sebastian*, II. i)

I believe that between the two modes of Augustan verse there exists a relation more organic than the dichotomy between official poetry and play poetry seems to propose. It is not enough to say—although it is true —that without Dryden's *Aeneid* Pope's *Rape of the Lock* could not have been written in its present form; for the *Aeneid* was more than a mere "source" for some of Pope's rhetoric or imagery. The burlesque mode so much admired, and so justly admired, among Pope and Dryden's twentieth-century critics clearly depended for its force on the very world view—clear, reasonable, orderly, moral—that it inverted or twisted askew. You can make interesting fragments out of a smashed statue, but not out of a smashed mudpie. Furthermore, the positive values which gave a cutting edge to Augustan burlesque were not by any means things wholly and solely existing in the remote past, in distant cultures, in the giant age before the flood. On the contrary, they were incorporated in lively, if sometimes dilute or concentrated, form in the poetry, both burlesque and "official," of the Augustans themselves; and they were incorporated in it with varying degrees of genuine esthetic success, some of which I hope have been illustrated in the foregoing essay on Dryden's translations. Pope's surrealistic evocation of Timon's gardens—

> The suffering eye inverted Nature sees,
> Trees cut to Statues, Statues thick as trees;
> With here a Fountain, never to be played;
> And there a Summerhouse, that knows no shade;
> Here Amphitrite sails through myrtle bowers;
> There Gladiators fight, or die in flowers;
> Unwatered see the drooping sea-horse mourn,
> And swallows roost in Nilus' dusty Urn—

is not a poetic *alternative* to his subsequent magnificent vision, in the same poem, of the same property restored to an ideal norm:

> Another age shall see the golden Ear
> Embrown the Slope, and nod on the Parterre,
> Deep harvests bury all his pride has planned,
> And laughing Ceres reassume the land.

The two depend upon each other.

Index